n Here?

Alternatives

ical Nursing

Where Do I Go From Here?

Exploring Your Career Alternatives Within and Beyond Clinical Nursing

Betty Hafner, *MS, NCC*
National Certified Counselor

Lippincott
Philadelphia · New York · Baltimore

Acquisitions Editor: Alan Sorkowitz
Project Editor: Nicole Walz
Senior Production Manager: Helen Ewan
Managing Editor/Production: Barbara Ryalls
Art Director: Carolyn O'Brien
Design: Emily Betsch
Manufacturing Manager: William Alberti
Indexer: Gaye Taralla
Printer: R.R. Donnelley & Sons—Crawfordsville

9 8 7 6 5 4 3 2 1

Library of Congress Cataloging-in-Publication Data

Hafner Betty.
Where do I go from here? : exploring your career alternatives within and beyond clinical nursing / by Betty Hafner.
p. ; cm.
Includes bibliographical references and index
ISBN 0-7817-3492-4 (alk. paper)
1. Nursing--Vocational guidance. 2. Nurses--Employment. 3. Job hunting. I. Title.
[DNLM: 1. Nursing--United States. 2. Career Mobility--United States. WY 16 H139w 2002]
RT86.7 .H345 2002
610.73'06'9--dc21

2001029915

Care has been taken to confirm the accuracy of the information presented and to describe generally accepted practices. However, the authors, editors, and publisher are not responsible for errors or omissions or for any consequences from application of the information in this book and make no warranty, express or implied, with respect to the content of the publication.

The authors, editors, and publisher have exerted every effort to ensure that drug selection and dosage set forth in this text are in accordance with the current recommendations and practice at the time of publication. However, in view of ongoing research, changes in government regulations, and the constant flow of information relating to drug therapy and drug reactions, the reader is urged to check the package insert for each drug for any change in indications and dosage and for added warnings and precautions. This is particularly important when the recommended agent is a new or infrequently employed drug.

Some drugs and medical devices presented in this publication have Food and Drug Administration (FDA) clearance for limited use in restricted research settings. It is the responsibility of the health care provider to ascertain the FDA status of each drug or device planned for use in his or her clinical practice.

Reviewers

Nancy Duval, RN, BSN
Professional Healthcare Recruiter
Nursing Management Services
Marietta, Georgia

Nancy Girard, PhD, RN
Associate Professor and Chair, Acute Nursing Care Department
University of Texas Health Science Center at San Antonio
San Antonio, Texas

Michael McDaniel, PhD
Associate Professor
School of Business
Virginia Commonwealth University
Richmond, Virginia

Kathryn B. Reid, RN, MSN, CCRN, FNP
Instructor of Nursing
University of Virginia School of Nursing
Charlottesville, Virginia

Carol R. Singer, RN, BSN, CSN
Certified School Nurse
Camden City Board of Education
Camden, New Jersey

Foreword

WE PARTICIPATED IN A FOCUS GROUP OF NURSES WHICH WAS ASKED, "WHAT WOULD A nurse find valuable in this book?" Our conversation first centered on the nursing options presented; the exploration of our traits, skills, and qualities as they relate to nursing; the stories and perceptions of so many nurses; the confidence-boosting tone; the forward-thinking approach; and the discussions of risk taking, change, and growth.

But that doesn't tell the whole story. The book also allows the reader to think "out-of-the-box", bringing us to a place where we can envision nursing as "something else"—something other than what it is traditionally known to be. The timing for this book couldn't be more appropriate. Some would say that this is a time of crisis within nursing. We are experiencing the biggest nursing shortage in the history of the profession. Many who remain in the profession are experiencing burnout, confusion, and the need to re-examine their options.

With the shift in health care to prevention and wellness, the growing nursing shortage and other recent changes, the opportunities for nurses are vast and are becoming more varied. With nurses in positions of leadership and management; in autonomous practices; in educational and consultation roles, the doors for growth and change have swung wide open. This book provides the first glance into this new world of nursing, beyond medication administration and direct patient care. It not only opens the doors but is written to guide us along our journey.

At a certain age or a certain point in your career it is natural to question your skills and wonder whether you possess something that is still valued. The book says, "Yes!"; your skills are valuable and so are you. It is a self-esteem booster, giving you the confidence to move ahead. The vignettes are inspirational. They let you know that it is not just talk; there are actually people out there doing what you might have always wanted to do and they are successful at it. At some point in their lives they were at the same crossroads ... wanting to change, wanting to experiment, wanting to test the waters, and they too, were hesitant and scared, and guess what? They made it! One nurse said that the book makes change seem possible and makes the options real ... "It gives me the courage to step out there on a ledge, since others have done it and have succeeded."

The book affords you the opportunity to re-examine your daily tasks—how you feel about what you do and whether you are just going through the motions. It forces you to account for the skills you have. Within the profession, you often hear nurses say, "Oh, I'm just a nurse". We devalue what we do. This book makes it clear that we are more than "just a nurse". We see that nursing can open the floodgates to endless opportunities for growth and fulfillment. It is one of the few professions, where you don't necessarily have to "fit a job"; it is more an issue of the job fitting you ... your likes, your preferences, your skills, your joys, your vision. When we talk to nurses doing innovative, creative things and we ask, "How did you get here?", they often say "Oh, I just stumbled into this". It is as if they had no plan. In reality, there was a plan. They had made a decision at some point to move, to change, to take a risk, to try, and as their confidence grew, their ability to envision success grow; and an expert was born. That's how they got where they are. We need to acknowledge the value of our skills, abilities, and intent and not accept things as a coincidence. This book reminds us of that.

Where Do I Go From Here? is not only for "first-degree", experienced nurses, though. It would serve as a great tool for those known as "second-degree nurses"—individuals coming into the profession from various backgrounds including, business, accounting and law, for example, who bring a wealth of professional and life experiences. This book is a must for their reading list.

Whether you are a new grad trying to find your "fit" or an experienced nurse who is asking "Is this what I really want to continue doing?", you'll find something valuable here.

—Sherry Higgins, RN, MSN
—Brigitte O'Halloran, RN, MS
—Joanne Johnson, RN

Preface

IF YOU'RE A NURSE CONSIDERING A CAREER MOVE, YOU'VE PICKED THE RIGHT BOOK. Whether you're simply curious about your alternatives or fiercely determined to choose one, you can find help in these pages. When writing it, I had in mind nurses who are

- looking for a new challenge
- developing different talents and interests
- dealing with a change in their family lives
- feeling unfulfilled professionally
- beginning careers in nursing
- coming into the field as second-degree nurses
- returning to nursing after time away
- contemplating retirement
- coming to the US from another country

No matter what your motivation is, you'll get *encouragement* about how valuable *and* transferable your nursing experience is. You'll also get *ideas* for new directions to take or ways to enrich your career as you learn what other nurses have done. You'll find here, too, a clear-cut *strategy* for making a change in your work life. And finally, the book offers you a way to find *work that's right for you.*

If the book sounds like it has a counseling slant to it, it should. I've been a career and educational counselor for more than 25 years. I developed a special interest in nurses and their career issues years ago while giving adult education workshops in Florida. One of my programs presented alternative careers for teachers and social workers, and my supervisor, a former nurse, once suggested I include nurses in it. I did just that the next semester, and from that point on, they filled the classes.

These practicing nurses presented me with the challenge of learning how they might use their skills outside patient care but also find the personal and professional satisfaction that it offers them. I found little written material to guide me on alternatives for nurses and discovered that the only reliable way to gather information was to ask nurses who had found out for themselves. To create a list of nurses I could question, I called scores of associations and organizations for leads, networked with nurses, read newsletters and periodicals, talked to managers of human resource departments, scanned directories, and contacted schools of nursing. This first group then referred me to others, and over time I collected information from more than 175 nurses. I wrote up some early findings in *The Nurse's Guide to Starting a Small Business* (Pilot Books, 1992), which featured those who took the entrepreneurial route.

The stories in this book of nurses who've shifted gears are sure to inspire you. I cast a wide net to find them—young and old, male and female, from Alaska to Florida. (I've used the feminine pronoun throughout, however, because of the overwhelming majority of females in the profession.) The nurses you'll meet are regular people but role models all the same. They've taken the career they've chosen and made it work for them. I asked them to tell me why they changed, what the new work involves, where they got help, and what rewards they're finding. You'll also learn from them the many ways they made their moves—some nurses applied for already existing positions while others literally created their new work and still others were drafted to fill a role they'd prepared themselves for. Each story has something to teach about courage or perseverance or timing or common sense.

I've used a workshop format for the book so you can process the material as you read it. In Section 1, I'll give you guidelines for viewing your options with a positive mind set. In Section 2, I'll ask you to identify specifics about your personal qualities, your background, your circumstances, and your goals that will help you make good decisions. If you do the exercises, you'll leave this section with a valuable summary sheet. Then in Section 3, you'll hear about nurses who've made moves within clinical nursing. In Section 4, you'll learn more about your options by examining what others are doing beyond clinical care. At the end of each chapter in Section 3 and 4, I'll ask you to think about whether that's the right direction for you, and suggest ways to follow up on it if you're interested. Finally, Section 5 takes you through a seven-step process that will get you ready for a change. Throughout the book you can choose how actively you participate, but I highly recommend that you do the exercises, record your results, and write responses to the questions asked. You'll get so much more out of it.

All along the way, I hope you'll hear the supportive, encouraging voice of someone who believes you have an enormously valuable background to share and any number of ways to share it. I hope you have fun sorting through your options.

Acknowledgments

I WOULD LIKE TO THANK ALL OF THE NURSES WHO SHARED THEIR STORIES WITH ME. They answered my questions willingly, good-naturedly, and fully showing a genuine interest in helping others make decisions. Their stories bring life to the book.

My thanks also goes to many others who played a role in the preparation of the book. Sherril L. Ingram, BSN, MS, DNSc; Deidre A. Krause, PhD, ARNP, CS; and Barbara Ross, BSN, MSN, EdD were valued consultants and reviewers on an earlier draft of the book. Ellyn Cavanaugh, RN; Sonja Simpson, RN; Janet Ladd, RN; and Vivien Butler, RN, LMT provided feedback, support, or ideas at just the right time. My enthusiastic local focus group—Brigitte O'Halloran, RN, MS; Sherry Higgins, RN, MSN; Ellen Hellawell, RNC; Pat Hanley; and Joanne Johnson, RN—played the important role of sounding board for me. Ruth Gruen, Robert Ungeleiter, and Melanie Freely were early supporters of this project and helped shape it. A final thank-you goes to my editor, Alan Sorkowitz, who handles everything with intelligence, professionalism, and a sense of humor.

Contents

section one

Preparing for a Change

Preparing for a Change

"It's an exciting time to be a nurse."

I hear that often from nurses these days. Even an old friend who was telling me about her niece recognized it. "She's finishing up her degree in nursing this year," she said, "Lucky kid. The world is her oyster."

It's not only brand new nurses who have so many exciting jobs to choose from and so many places they can go. All nurses, no matter what their experience is, can look forward to a future full of possibilities, and the more background you have in nursing, the more plentiful the options.

This book will guide you along a path where you'll explore your alternatives.

- ☐ You'll learn more about yourself and what it takes to create your ideal situation.
- ☐ You'll see how other nurses are using their experience to take up new roles.
- ☐ You'll weigh your various options using data gathered in the exercises.
- ☐ You'll find out how to develop your own action plan when you're ready to make a move.

To get the most of this process, you'll want to approach it with the right attitude. If your expectations are unrealistic, you could easily become disillusioned. If your awareness about how careers develop is incomplete, you could miss ideas or opportunities that are staring you in the face. If you put too much pressure on yourself or become judgmental about your desire to change, you may find it hard to move ahead. So before we move on, I ask you to consider these six positive ways to view your alternatives. I hope you'll take them to heart.

1. The Changes in Health Care Are Creating Opportunities

You've all been in some way affected by the recent changes in the delivery of health care. The industry is in a state of flux; health care dollars are shrinking and HMOs and insurance companies seem to be calling the shots. New models of management are being put in place that, nurses say, often seem to be misguided. While thankful for the ongoing, steady stream of innovative medical technology, we're learning that its high cost has taxed hospital budgets and taken away from other things that nurses feel are priorities.

Many of the nurses I interviewed for this book voiced a discontent with their work. They told me—loudly and clearly—"things just aren't the same." Again and again I heard the refrains,

"It's not like it used to be."
"I don't have time to do my job."
"It's not possible to give patients the kind of care they need."

Some were frustrated by the changes in hospital nursing and the roles they now must play. Others said they felt lost or, at the very least, off track.

The result of these and other developments is that nurses are now working in hospitals and other facilities that are merging, downsizing, and restructuring. The stress of this situation has made it hard for many nurses to be comfortable, contributing workers in today's hospitals and health care agencies. Nurses who expressed dissatisfaction also felt that their job description is changing and that they're now given a greater patient load. To compound the problem, the move toward shortened hospital stays and a push toward outpatient care has escalated the acuity level of patients.

This has created a challenging situation for nurses trying to do quality work. The bottom line is that acute care nursing may no longer be the right answer for some professional nurses.

It's natural to react negatively to change; we lose our equilibrium and miss the structure of the status quo. But, although some people may get stuck in a negative, complaining mode, *you* don't have to. There's a positive side to the changes in health care. These changes are opening doors for you. If, for example, you were to list some of the newer developments in health care, you might mention:

- Shorter hospital stays for patients
- More outpatient care
- Greater decision-making responsibilities for insurance companies
- Emphasis on cost-effective treatment
- More accountability demanded of providers
- Wider acceptance of complementary and alternative treatments
- Increased emphasis on wellness and prevention

Look at the way these developments point to new opportunities for nurses.

- Nurses are moving in greater numbers into ambulatory care centers, community clinics, rehabilitation facilities, and home health care agencies.
- They are working as case managers, playing an important role in the efficient delivery of care.
- They are becoming quality or performance improvement professionals.
- They are becoming practitioners of alternative methods of care in a number of settings.
- They are entering the burgeoning areas of wellness and preventative care by teaching, counseling, and writing.

This is just a sampling of possibilities that come out of the new business of health care. You'll see many more in later chapters.

2. You Can Design a Life That's Just Right for You.

Do you want to work 3 days a week and spend the other days revamping your screenplay? That's what a nurse in California does. Do you want to travel to the sunny South in winter and the mountains in summer? That's how a Florida couple sets up their traveling nursing assignments. Do you want to spend the weekdays with your young children and work only on weekends, when your spouse is home? That's just what many nurses report they do.

Statistics show that we've become a nation of freelancers, part-timers, contractors, and temps, and many people—including nurses—are working in whole new ways these days, piecing together short-term or part-time assignments and freelance jobs to create an interesting, diverse work life.

The changes in the way we do business also are opening doors for inventive nurses who are aware of their skills and areas of proficiency and have the confidence to promote their services and share their expertise. More and more small companies can't afford a staff of experts, so they hire consultants for special projects on a contractual basis. This trend toward outsourcing, as it's called, is an opportunity for nurses to work for short periods of time as a consultant to an agency, institution, or company.

Most businesses or facilities don't have their own education departments. Would you consider becoming a freelance teacher or trainer, hired for a specific task? Would you be comfortable forgoing a long-term commitment?

If you've uncovered a need that's not being addressed, might you want to set up a business and provide a service or product you know well?

You don't have to *wait* for a good job to open up. Many observant, imaginative nurses are creating their own jobs. Dive into the exercises in the next section and create a picture of your ideal life. It will give you something to work toward.

3. Your Next Move Might Be the First of Many.

Don't pressure yourself to find the perfect job for the rest of your life.

Good short-term decisions can help careers develop over time. This was evident to a number of the nurses I interviewed. Some who were very enthusiastic about what they were doing were noticing related work that intrigued them.

For example, a nurse who left hospital work to become a school nurse enjoys the counseling aspect of her job, so she is beginning psychology classes with the idea of someday counseling in another setting.

Another former staff nurse took a clinical job in a retirement community and, because of her advocacy work with seniors, is researching the field of medical-legal consulting.

A hospital human resource recruiter, who relishes matching health care workers and hospital jobs, thinks about someday becoming an outplacement generalist, helping to find situations for unemployed executives in different industries.

A nurse who, while doing intravenous equipment sales discovered how much she likes getting out and meeting people, is now selling real estate part time.

Another nurse, who found her calling in pharmaceutical sales is now a political lobbyist, selling her cause rather than a product line.

These nurses, while doing work they enjoyed, developed related interests that will take their careers in different directions. Their stories demonstrate how careers develop.

4. You Can Make a Difference and a Dollar.

I was three-quarters of the way through research for the book before anyone mentioned the forbidden subject: money. I don't mean specific sums of money; I mean *any* discussion of what people were earning or wanted to earn. (I guess I'm a polite, helping professional, so I didn't ask either.) The nurse who finally broke the barrier worked as a sales staff trainer for a company. In describing a friend and colleague who sells medical equipment, she offhandedly finished a thought with: "Oh, and she makes gobs of money." She said it so quietly I had to ask her to repeat it.

The nurse-turned-sales trainer told me more. "Our best sales people are nurses," she reported about her medical equipment company. "They're way on top of the game. We have tons of very successful nurses." As she explained it, the nurses on the sales force have a bond with their customers. It's not forced or rehearsed; it's real. What is obvious to all is that they are motivated by the desire to go into the health facility and *help*. The money just seems to follow.

Why are some nurses uncomfortable with the idea of making a lot of money? Perhaps it runs counter to what they feel they're all about. They are nurturers, helpers, and care givers. Nurturers don't usually charge a lot of money for their services, and our society certainly doesn't offer it to them. But that doesn't mean one can't be a first-rate care giver *and* earn enough to live well.

I spoke to many nurses who had lucrative careers in health care, business, and law, and they explained how they got past this stumbling block. *These nurses did not abandon the idea of being a helping professional.* Rather, they saw the work they did, whether it was in information systems, performance improvement, or insurance law, as helping patients get more efficient service, a higher quality of care, or a more just resolution of a problem. Just because you're in one of the helping professions, don't assume you can't make a big contribution to people's lives and be well paid for it.

5. Restlessness Happens. Don't Be Judgmental.

The sense that it's time to move on can strike us at any time. It can happen when we first take a job and learn what it's all about, only to realize that it's not for us. Or after years of doing the same work, it can become clear that we've lost the passion for it we once had. It can happen as our families grow and we need more time and energy for them. Or it can happen as we develop other parts of ourselves and want more creativity or responsibility or fun in our days. We humans are evolving creatures, and a need to change happens to nurses as it happens to everyone, but people in helping professions often carry the baggage of guilt—a voice that says "I shouldn't want to leave." It's important that you set aside the shoulds or should nots and look clearly at your circumstances.

A nurse manager asked me to give readers permission to consider leaving nursing if that's what they felt was right for them. She said she comes across nurses who don't belong in patient care and know it but feel an underlying pressure to stay. I hope the self-assessment exercises will help you identify and follow through with what's right for you.

Whatever the motivation for a career change, the wish remains the same: I found that nurses want to do something that will fit in with their lifestyles, give them something to look forward to each day, and let them feel they are contributing to the betterment of people's lives. And they're entitled to the quest for it.

6. You Don't Have to Go Far to Find What You're Seeking.

When I set out to organize my research on career alternatives for nurses, I noticed patterns emerging in the choices made by the professionals I interviewed. Of course, I heard about the occasional individual whose choice did not fit the patterns:

- a California nurse who's a salesperson in a family architectural and design company;
- a Pennsylvania nurse who built a successful gourmet mustard business;
- an Oregon nurse who sells her intricate sculptures of horses.

Leaving nursing and health care altogether *is* an option, but the overwhelming majority of nurses who leave their jobs end up capitalizing on their years of nursing experience in some way and working in or around health care.

Sections 3 and 4 will show you the directions taken by 120 of the nurses I interviewed.

- They chose different options in direct care that energized them.
- They found other specialized jobs within the domain of nursing.
- They went into alternative or complementary care.
- They started a small business, often ones that were related to health care.

- They entered a different profession, bringing with them knowledge of the nursing process.
- They worked on the business side of health care.

Whether or not they stayed in a health care facility, they brought their nursing skills and experience along, drew from it regularly, and were able to see their work as improving the lives of others.

So be aware of what is going on around you, in your facility and in health care in general. Talk with colleagues; read newspapers, journals, and periodicals; stay active in associations; and volunteer for working committees. You may find you don't have to look too far to find your own new direction.

Now you're ready to take a good look at what's important to you; discover what qualities, skills, and special knowledge you could bring to the work place; and define your ideal work. Enjoy the exercises that follow. They're all about you.

section two

Do a Self-Assessment

chapter 1

Take a Good Look

Getting Ready

WHEN YOU GET TO THE NEXT SECTION WHERE YOU'LL READ ABOUT THE DOZENS OF new ways nurses are working, you'll probably find yourself asking the question, "Would this work for me?" The exercises in the next three chapters will encourage you to draw a complete picture of what *will* work for you. You'll be looking at

- your motivation for changing jobs;
- your significant life values;
- the personality traits that affect your approach to life and work;
- your interests and areas of expertise;
- the skills you bring to your job; and
- the factors that make a setting ideal for you.

After each exercise, you'll write a Summary Statement that will help you identify the most important findings from that exercise. Your Summary Statements, when viewed together, will suggest possible paths for you to explore as well as provide you with an inspiring list of your strengths and accomplishments to refer to in the course of your career change.

You'll also notice Brainstorming Questions after each exercise, referred to in this manner because they are meant to stir your thinking in unexpected ways. Your answers to these questions provide a bridge between the exercises and the specific career directions you'll learn about later in the book. If you're working on the exercises with a group of friends or classmates, the Brainstorming Questions will be a good starting point for your discussions. Some of you might use them to inspire expanded, reflective journal entries.

As you complete each exercise in this section, collect the information from the Summary Statement that follows and record it on your Career Guidelines form on page 46. You'll be much closer to recognizing the types of jobs that will be satisfying to you when you look at this finished product.

If you're not able to complete the exercises on the pages of this book, use another method for recording the answers and conclusions. Although I refer to it as your "journal," it certainly doesn't have to be anything fancy. Personally, I favor the unused portion of my son's neon-green spiral notebooks. Lined paper usually is easier for recording, but whatever works for you is fine. Use a new page for each exercise or segment you complete, and be sure to note what is at the top of the page so you can go back to it as you move along. To make things easier to interpret and reference, put your Summary Statements on a separate page at the back of your journal so they all appear together. You should allow three pages or so for this section. Alternatively, you might want to use a computer database to collect the information as you work.

Ready? Let's begin.

exercise 1

The "Little Picture"

We first need to focus on the moment. Where are you right now in your thinking about your career? For starters, we know you're wondering about your career options because you're reading a book that gives you ideas for new work. But how committed are you to a change, and how much of a change are you willing to make? Do you have any ideas that you'd like to check out, or are you open to any and all suggestions? It's important to clarify your thinking about these issues.

If you were taking a workshop, the teacher might begin by going around the room and having each participant say why she was there. If you're like most people, your hands would start sweating, and you'd be too busy practicing what you were going to say to actually listen to what your classmates had to say. The pressure is off here, so just relax and answer the questions honestly.

[1.] I would describe myself as

- ☐ Just interested in looking around
- ☐ Planning to make a change in ______________ (months or years) or another time frame ___________________ (eg, when my child starts school)
- ☐ Ready to make a change as soon as possible

[2.] I would consider

- ☐ Staying at my current job with some changes
- ☐ A different setting for patient care
- ☐ A nursing function other than direct care
- ☐ A non-nursing job in health care
- ☐ Using my nursing background outside of health care
- ☐ Doing something unrelated to health care

[3.] What drew me to nursing?

____

____

____

[4.] When have I felt most happy at work?

____

____

____

[5.] Which of my work activities stimulate me?

____

____

____

[6.] Which of my work activities drain me?

____

____

____

[7.] If I could change only one thing about my job, what would it be?

____

____

____

[8.] Who does work I might like? What is appealing about it?

____

____

____

Summary Statement

Write a complete sentence summarizing your thoughts. Try to bring together some of the insights you gained from these questions.

For example, based on her answers, someone might summarize like this: "I would like to find work as soon as possible in a different patient-care setting where I won't have as much paperwork or unannounced overtime."

Another reader, looking at her responses, might say, "I would like a less physically demanding job performing a function other than direct care within the next 6 months."

See what you come up with.

I would like

___

___

___

You're on the way to clarifying your thinking about a career change.

Brainstorming Questions

How committed am I to staying in some type of health care position?

___

___

___

Did I find that I'm interested in several directions, or am I more focused?

___

___

___

Will any of my choices require me to take a big risk? How could I prepare for that?

___

___

___

These exercises are meant to help you decide what role you want work to play in your life and what kind of work you might like. As you explore your alternatives, keep in mind the major goals of your life or what we're calling the "big picture."

exercise 2

The "Big Picture"

The next exercise is a lot of fun because it asks you to look into the future and create that future any way you want, as long as you stay within the boundaries of logical possibility. Here's how: pretend you're a journalist writing a short piece honoring you on the occasion of your 100th birthday. Think about what the journalist might include—remarks about your work, family, education, accomplishments, talents, interests, personality, or anything else that's appropriate. See what you come up within a couple of paragraphs.

Summary Statement

To write your Summary Statement, reread your article, looking for the things that you expect will give meaning to your life. Refer to the list below for ideas in completing your statement.

What is important to me? (Pick three or four.)

- ☐ Close family ties
- ☐ Personal growth

- ☐ Spirituality
- ☐ Personal relationships
- ☐ Independence
- ☐ Helping others
- ☐ Financial success
- ☐ Leadership, being influential
- ☐ Professional achievement
- ☐ Gaining knowledge
- ☐ Having experiences
- ☐ Using talents
- ☐ Other ______________________

Write your response below or in your journal.

The qualities that make my life meaningful are

____

____

____

Brainstorming Question

If I were able to write only one sentence summing up my life, what would I want to include?

____

____

____

Keep your pencil handy. There's more to consider.

chapter 2

Discover What You Have to Offer

IN THE LAST CHAPTER, YOU THOUGHT ABOUT HOW YOU VIEW YOUR WORK. You first looked at what type of change you were considering, and then you thought about what you value in your work and in other aspects of your life. Now let's focus on what you bring to your work. Your special collection of personality traits, skills, interests, knowledge, and experiences has a lot to do with the kind of work you choose. You probably chose your current or most recent nursing job because you saw it as a good fit for you. But since starting it, you've most likely grown, accumulated a number of skills, and had a variety of professional experiences. Now new possibilities are opening for you.

Knowing which new direction to take becomes a challenge. There's no chart in existence that will match all of your assets with the right job. Your work is multifaceted, and your personal life is filled with considerations that affect your choice of work. You have to put the pieces together yourself, and the way to do that is

- get a clear understanding of what you have to offer;
- be aware of what you need from your work; and
- learn as much as you can about your career options.

The next four exercises will help you with the first task. You'll look at your special personal qualities and the skills, interests, and experiences that enrich you as a person and a professional.

exercise 3

Personal Qualities

Think of how you are viewed by those closest to you. If your family and friends had to put together a report card for you, what might they say? Check off the positive qualities that best describe you or list them on a new page of your journal.

- ☐ adaptable
- ☐ adventurous
- ☐ alert
- ☐ ambitious
- ☐ analytical
- ☐ artistic
- ☐ assertive
- ☐ calm
- ☐ capable
- ☐ cautious
- ☐ cheerful
- ☐ clever
- ☐ compassionate
- ☐ competent
- ☐ competitive
- ☐ confident
- ☐ conscientious
- ☐ controlled
- ☐ cooperative
- ☐ courageous
- ☐ creative
- ☐ curious
- ☐ dedicated
- ☐ deliberate
- ☐ dependable
- ☐ determined
- ☐ efficient
- ☐ empathic
- ☐ energetic
- ☐ enterprising
- ☐ extroverted
- ☐ flexible
- ☐ focused
- ☐ frank
- ☐ friendly
- ☐ good-natured
- ☐ healthy
- ☐ helpful
- ☐ honest
- ☐ humorous
- ☐ idealistic
- ☐ imaginative
- ☐ independent
- ☐ industrious
- ☐ intellectual
- ☐ intelligent
- ☐ introverted
- ☐ intuitive
- ☐ logical
- ☐ mature
- ☐ methodical
- ☐ modest
- ☐ nonjudgmental
- ☐ observant
- ☐ open
- ☐ opportunistic
- ☐ organized
- ☐ outgoing
- ☐ patient
- ☐ persevering
- ☐ persuasive
- ☐ practical
- ☐ precise
- ☐ quick study
- ☐ quiet
- ☐ rational
- ☐ reasonable
- ☐ reflective
- ☐ reserved
- ☐ resourceful
- ☐ responsible
- ☐ scholarly

- ☐ self-confident
- ☐ self-motivated
- ☐ sensitive
- ☐ serious
- ☐ sociable
- ☐ spontaneous
- ☐ strong-willed
- ☐ sympathetic
- ☐ tactful
- ☐ team player
- ☐ tenacious
- ☐ thorough
- ☐ thoughtful
- ☐ tolerant
- ☐ trustworthy
- ☐ unaffected
- ☐ understanding
- ☐ verbal
- ☐ versatile
- ☐ warm
- ☐ willing to take risks

Summary Statement

Select the five traits that best describe you. Record your completed statement below or in your journal.

I can be described as

____

____

____

____

Brainstorming Questions

Which qualities have a definite impact on the way I work?

____

____

____

Which qualities would I most want to use in my work?

exercise 4

Special Interests

Let's look at the ways you like to spend your leisure time. What interests you, excites you? Creating a list of these interests or hobbies may help you explore career ideas because they could become the seed for a new job or your own small business.

Answer the following questions to help you make up this list or write your responses on a separate sheet of your journal. These also work well as discussion questions for group work.

- What's my favorite way of spending a weekend afternoon?

- What did I do on lazy, rainy afternoons as a child?

- What do I like to do on vacation?

- What magazines do I subscribe to or regularly buy?

- What adult education courses have I taken or considered taking?

- What section of the newspaper do I most enjoy reading?

- What type of nonfiction book attracts me?

- What kind of TV shows do I most enjoy?

- Do I collect anything or admire any kind of collections?

- What volunteer activities am I involved in or have I considered doing?

- Am I a member of any nonprofessional organization(s)? What are they?

______

______

______

- In what kind of store do I enjoy browsing?

______

______

______

- What would I like to do that I haven't done yet?

______

______

______

Summary Statement

Your summary statement should list the answers that describe your meaningful interests. Don't delete your strong likes because you can't see how they might fit into a work setting. This list simply outlines things that you enjoy. If they fit and how they fit into your career plans remain to be seen. Write your response below or on the summary page of your journal.

(Example: "I like reading self-help books, taking classes on financial planning, and volunteering with retired people.")

I like ______

______

______

______

Brainstorming Questions

Would I like to spend more time on any of my interests? Which one(s)?

____

____

____

Do I have interests that I would definitely like to incorporate into my work?

____

____

____

____

In the new directions I'm considering, will there still be time to do the things I like?

____

____

____

____

exercise 5

Areas of Expertise

This next exercise is a self-esteem booster. It will remind you of things you've studied, learned, and experienced during your lifetime. It also will serve as a list of your career interests because in many cases you chose your learning experiences. You'll want to take these areas of expertise into account as you explore work opportunities and promote them, where appropriate, in a résumé or interview if you're seeking a new job. As you go through the book, come back to this exercise and add items as they occur to you.

Note the following achievements here or in your journal.

My major or area of concentration in college was

____

____

____

____

My major area of concentration in graduate school was

____

____

____

I have

- ☐ Specialty certification(s): ______________________________

  ____

  ____

  ____

- ☐ Special equipment training: ______________________________

  ____

  ____

  ____

- ☐ Technology training: ______________________________

  ____

  ____

  ____

- ☐ Specialized work experience: ______________________________

  ____

  ____

  ____

☐ Special life experiences: ______________________________

____

____

____

☐ Knowledge of foreign language(s): ______________________________

____

____

____

☐ Significant knowledge of another culture: ______________________________

____

____

____

☐ Other ______________________________

____

____

____

I have taken the following:

☐ Seminars:

____

____

____

☐ Workshops:

____

____

____

☐ In-services:

____

____

____

☐ Adult education courses:

____

____

____

____

Summary Statement

Put a check next to the items that you currently think will be most meaningful to you in your work and then list them below. This may change as you continue to explore.

I am knowledgeable about

____

____

____

____

Brainstorming Questions

Would I like a job that centered on any areas I mentioned?

____

____

____

____

Would I like to teach in my areas of expertise?

____

____

____

____

Would I be able to act as a consultant in any areas where I have an expertise?

___

___

___

___

Could any of my expertise become the basis of a small business?

___

___

___

___

Are there any specialized areas I might enjoy learning more about?

___

___

___

___

exercise 6

Transferable Skills

Take your time with this next exercise, it's a crucial one. After working on it, the contributions you can make to any setting will become clearer, and you'll have a list of dynamic words you can use as you promote yourself in conversation or in writing.

In the previous exercise, you listed some of the technical, mechanical, and nursing skills you've acquired through specialty education. But some of your most important talents are shown in the way you handle people or manage your work, and these talents are harder to pinpoint.

The next exercise will help you identify these interpersonal and functional skills. Nothing will give you better information about yourself, make you feel more positive about your skills and accomplishments, or better prepare you to talk to others about what you can offer them on the job.

So pick up a pencil and five pieces of paper or your journal. Sit back, relax, and think of five successful situations you've been involved in, in or out of work, where you accomplished something you were proud of (you might find the nonwork situations especially helpful because you'll have had more choice about the role you played). Select situations that will show interpersonal and functional skills, rather than, let's say, physical or artistic ones, although such skills are important. On each of the five pages, describe one situation; write a paragraph stating exactly what you did to carry out this activity. Make sure to focus on the actions you took, relying heavily on verbs.

When you've finished with these five paragraphs, turn to the list that follows, and for each situation, read through the verbs in the column labeled Your Actions. Each time you find a verb that describes what you did in that particular situation, check it off under the situation number. We'll pull it all together when you finish. See what you come up with (Table 2-1).

Now, reviewing this list of verbs, look for patterns. In which marketable skill areas do you find a lot of your accomplishments? In your summary statement, you'll make note of these marketable skills and specific actions.

Summary Statement

You can repeat the sentence below for as many of the marketable skill groups as you want. Read through these examples first and follow the pattern.

> I am skilled in Program Development and Management because I *created* and *implemented* a triage program (No. 1), *devised* and *implemented* a patient satisfaction survey (No. 1) and *organized* the development of a countywide disaster program (No. 2).

or

TABLE 2-1.

Marketable Skills	Your Action	No. 1	No. 2	No. 3	No. 4	No. 5
Program development	Created					
	Designed					
	Developed					
	Produced					
	Planned					
	Initiated					
	Generated					
	Visualized					
	Revised					
Management/ Organizational	Delegated					
	Scheduled					
	Arranged					
	Organized					
	Set goals					
	Facilitated					
	Managed					
	Administered					
	Conducted					
	Selected					
	Implemented					
	Performed					
	Devised					
	Improved					

continues

Marketable Skills	Your Action	No. 1	No. 2	No. 3	No. 4	No. 5
Leadership	Inspired					
	Chaired					
	Supervised					
	Directed					
	Led					
	Oversaw					
Human Relations	Advised					
	Counseled					
	Encouraged					
	Motivated					
	Collaborated					
	Recruited					
	Mediated					
	Advocated					
	Empathized					
Communications	Consulted					
	Interviewed					
	Facilitated					
	Communicated					
	Explained					
	Listened					
	Debated					
	Negotiated					
	Resolved					
	Spoke publicly					

continues

Marketable Skills	Your Action	No. 1	No. 2	No. 3	No. 4	No. 5
Written communications	Recorded					
	Corresponded					
	Reported					
	Reviewed					
	Wrote					
	Documented					
	Composed					
Education/ Training	Instructed					
	Taught					
	Trained					
	Mentored					
	Presented					
	Lectured					
	Explained					
	Demonstrated					
	Conducted					
	Translated					
Marketing/ Sales	Advertised					
	Promoted					
	Sold					
	Persuaded					
	Influenced					
	Developed relationships					
	Raised Funds					

continues

Marketable Skills	Your Action	No. 1	No. 2	No. 3	No. 4	No. 5
Analysis/ Research	Investigated					
	Reported					
	Compiled					
	Researched					
	Summarized					
	Analyzed					
	Interpreted					
	Calculated					
	Discovered					
	Simplified					
	Assessed					

I am skilled in *Marketing and Sales* because I have *raised funds* for a church choir trip (No. 3), *advertised* and *sold* a house by myself (No. 4), and *promoted* and *sold* a line of accessories from my home (No. 5). I am skilled in ____________________ because I have _______________

____

____

____

Brainstorming Questions

In what areas am I the most skilled?

____

____

____

____

Which skills would I most like to use in my work?

____

____

____

____

The next three exercises will take you from a focus on yourself to a focus on the work environment that will be satisfying to you. You'll become more aware of what you need from your work. These exercises are quick but full of useful information. Don't skip them.

chapter 3

Be Clear About Your Ideal Work

IN THE LAST CHAPTER YOU LOOKED AT YOUR PERSONAL TRAITS, INTERESTS, KNOWLEDGE, and skills. Your next task is to flesh out some of the details of your ideal work: What would this job look like? You're going to be called upon to be demanding, and you might be reluctant to do so at first. People often worry that they're being too picky and that they're eliminating too many possibilities. You, of course, *will* be eliminating many, but so much the better. You'll be left with the characteristics that point you in the direction of the settings that work for you.

exercise 7

People Preferences

Nurses are drawn to their work because of the high level of contact with people. I know. When I asked more than 100 of them why they went into nursing, they all said, in some way, "I wanted to help people." But just because you're a people person, doesn't necessarily mean you would choose to help all types of people, all of the time. We all have our preferences. There are certain people we're especially gifted with or drawn to and others we don't work particularly well with.

Because most nurses—even when making dramatic career changes—stay in fields where they're heavily involved with other people, this checklist will give you important information about how you react to various types of people and the work that involves them. You'll make note of your preferences in your Summary Statement and be able to take them into account as you explore career options.

One piece of advice: go through this exercise quickly. You'll learn more if you react quickly and check off as few or as many as you want. The list is meant to stimulate your thinking, but it may not be complete. If some other category comes to mind, be sure to add it.

I would like to work in a setting where I'm *primarily* helping

- ☐ A mix of ages
- ☐ Older adults
- ☐ Adults
- ☐ College students
- ☐ Teen-agers
- ☐ Children
- ☐ Babies
- ☐ Individuals, one-on-one
- ☐ People in groups
- ☐ Couples
- ☐ Families
- ☐ Parents
- ☐ Males
- ☐ Females

I would like *my focus* to be on people who

- ☐ are acutely ill
- ☐ have chronic conditions
- ☐ have ill family members
- ☐ are terminally ill
- ☐ have disabilities
- ☐ do not have pressing health issues
- ☐ are practicing nurses
- ☐ have experienced recent trauma
- ☐ have an addiction
- ☐ are pregnant
- ☐ have emotional/mental problems

- ☐ have marital/sexual problems
- ☐ have educational needs
- ☐ have career problems
- ☐ have business/financial concerns
- ☐ have legal problems
- ☐ are religious/spiritual
- ☐ come from a different culture
- ☐ are in the military
- ☐ are underserved
- ☐ Other __________

Summary Statement

To complete your statement, you'll need to go back and look over your responses to pick the groups you're most interested in working with. If you'd like, combine them in ways that reflect your feelings. Record them below or in your journal.

As an example, someone might say, "I would like to work with pregnant, disadvantaged women or teen-agers."

I would like to work with ______________________________

____

____

____

Brainstorming Questions

Do I have experience with the types of people I prefer to work with? If not, is there a way I could get experience in a volunteer or part-time situation?

____

____

____

Would I need additional education or training?

____

____

____

Could I talk to someone who works with these individuals?

____

____

____

exercise 8

Work Environments

For this exercise, first think about your past work experiences, paid or unpaid. What were their positive and negative aspects? What did you express as a negative about your current situation in Exercise 1? Think back to your school and college experiences. How did you react to schools of different size? How comfortable were you there? In *any* situation where you were required to be productive, how did you respond to the different atmospheres of the institutions and organizations? How did you find the different authority styles you came across? What was your reaction to the attitudes of your colleagues or classmates?

By suggesting different features that you might find in a work setting, this quick exercise will help you develop a list of those you'd like in an ideal situation. Read through the descriptions and check off any that appeal to you. Once again, list any other words that come to mind as you do this exercise.

I would like to work

- ☐ In a large organization
- ☐ In a medium size organization
- ☐ In a small organization
- ☐ With a few partners
- ☐ With one partner
- ☐ On my own

I prefer an environment that could be described as

- ☐ Predictable
- ☐ Changeable
- ☐ High tech
- ☐ Low tech
- ☐ Competitive
- ☐ Less competitive
- ☐ Academic
- ☐ Closely supervised
- ☐ Loosely supervised
- ☐ Flexible
- ☐ Fast paced
- ☐ Relaxed
- ☐ Other ___________

Now that you've reacted to the feel of the environment, check off the settings that interest you. Add any you'd like.

I would like to work in

- ☐ My home
- ☐ The homes of other people
- ☐ An acute-care facility
- ☐ A post-acute care facility
- ☐ A long-term care facility
- ☐ A professional office
- ☐ A community-based health care setting
- ☐ A variety of settings
- ☐ An academic/educational setting
- ☐ A legal setting
- ☐ A business office
- ☐ Other __________

Summary Statement

Once again, you'll need to go over the choices you made, pick the ones that are most important to you, and record your answers. Combine them if that works better for you. For example, someone might say, "I would like to work in a small, relaxed professional office with a few partners." What would you say?

I would like to work

___

___

___

Brainstorming Question

If I could choose only one quality, which would I pick? Why?

___

___

___

exercise 9

Wish List

In a previous chapter, you were asked to pinpoint why you might want to leave your current job. Did you come up with any requirements or responsibilities that don't suit your life now? In this exercise you'll get a chance to create a list of the things you *would* like to have in your ideal job.

The nurses I surveyed were very clear about what was important to them. Most of the qualities listed were those they mentioned at some point. Check the items that apply to you and be sure to add any you think of that were not mentioned.

I want work that has

- ☐ Flexible scheduling
- ☐ Definite hours
- ☐ Local travel
- ☐ Long-distance travel
- ☐ No travel
- ☐ Full-time hours
- ☐ Part-time hours
  - ☐ How many days per week? _____
  - ☐ How many hours per week? _____
- ☐ Weekend hours
- ☐ No weekend hours
- ☐ Night shifts
- ☐ No night shifts
- ☐ Minimum salary of _____
- ☐ Ideal salary of _____
- ☐ High degree of job security
- ☐ Short-term commitment only
- ☐ On-site child care
- ☐ On-site health/fitness facility
- ☐ Possibility of work at home
- ☐ Little or no physical work
- ☐ Other __________

Summary Statement

For this Summary Statement, list *every* item you checked off; after all, it's a "wish list." See if you can list them in their priority of importance to you. For example, someone might say, beginning with the most important first, "I would like a part-time job for 25 hours per week with flexible weekday and weekend scheduling, no night shifts, and local travel only."

What is important to you?

I would like ____

____

____

Brainstorming Question

Which ones of the characteristics that I've chosen are not negotiable? (Put a star next to each one.)

Use the Career Guidelines form that follows to collect your findings.

Career Guidelines

exercise 1

The 'Little Picture' (page 14)

I would like ____

____

____

____

exercise 2

The 'Big Picture' (page 18)

The qualities that make my life meaningful are ____________________

____

____

____

exercise 3

Personal Qualities (page 22)

I can be described as ______________________________

____

____

____

____

exercise 4

Special Interests (page 24)

I like ______________________________

____

____

____

____

exercise 5

Areas of Expertise (page 27)

I am knowledgeable about ______________________________

____

____

____

____

exercise 6

Transferable Skills (Page 31)

I am skilled in ______________________________

____

____

____

____

exercise 7

People Preferences (Page 39)

I would like to work with ______________________________

____

____

____

____

exercise 8

Work Environments (Page 42)

I would like to work in ______________________________

____

____

____

____

exercise 9

Wish List (Page 44)

I would like ______________________________

____

____

____

____

Now, with your Career Guidelines form in hand, you'll be ready to brainstorm with others about your next professional step. Nurses have found the following people to be especially helpful in suggesting and weighing different options. Who might be able to help you?

Nursing colleagues ______________________________

____

____

____

____

Former teachers ______________________________

____

____

____

____

Respected managers ______________________________

____

____

____

College/university career center counselors ______________________

____

____

____

Professional counselors ______________________________

____

____

____

The question you most likely want answered now is some version of "In what type of work would my skills, interests, expertise, and personal traits be valued and my preferences be possible?" Read through the next section with that question in mind. You'll get help answering this most pressing question as you learn from the experiences of other nurses and answer thoughtfully the questions that follow each chapter. The resources included at the end of the section will help connect you with other people who can describe in detail the work involved.

section three

Learn About Your Alternatives Within Clinical Nursing

chapter 4

Look at Different Options in Direct Care

FOR MANY NURSES, THE ANSWER TO THE QUESTION, "WHERE DO I GO FROM HERE?" is to be found in a new role in patient care. Yet many nurses talk of leaving before exploring all of their options within the profession. Margaret L., a Pennsylvania nurse, told me about two friends who dealt with their frustrations by leaving nursing completely. Although they both developed other careers in business, their stories don't have happy endings. "They both miss nursing terribly," Margaret told me, "so they do it part time, on weekends . . . like a hobby."

There are many reasons nurses choose to satisfy their need for a change by moving into a different area of patient care. They may

- find they're energized by the busy life of a clinician;
- enjoy the critical thinking and creative problem solving that's demanded of them each day;
- want to develop their nursing skills to gain more responsibility and respect;
- want more experience in patient care before branching into a different area;
- have concerns about giving up their current level of income; or
- thrive on the satisfaction of caring for people at their most vulnerable time.

One nurse I learned about dealt with her desire for change in a dramatic way. She was tired of hospital work but loved patient care. This self-directed nurse decided to energize her career by working with a different population in a different setting. She joined the Jesuit Volunteer Corps, packed her bags, and went to St. Mary's, Alaska. The town, at the time, consisted of about 300 Native Americans. She taught at the high school there and was the village nurse. As the most highly trained medical person in the village, she found herself diagnosing illnesses, handling emergencies, and prescribing medicines. It was exhausting and challenging and brought a renewed passion for nursing, which she continued when she returned home.

But you don't have to move to Alaska to find job satisfaction. Many nurses transform their work situation without leaving home for exotic locations. They might continue as a staff nurse but in a different department of their hospital. They might move into the community in a hemodialysis center or work with elderly Alzheimer's patients in an adult day care center. They might bring diversity into their work lives by traveling and changing their work setting every 6 months or so. The possibilities are endless.

Of the dozens of nurses I spoke with who handled their job dissatisfaction by making a change within patient care, all agreed the shift brought a renewed energy to their work. In the process they discovered new talents, achieved a higher degree of competency, and earned greater respect.

Remember, the ability to move around to such a broad variety of settings within the boundaries of clinical nursing is one of the most exciting aspects of your career.

You have a multitude of choices, with new ones developing all of the time. This chapter provides ideas about how you can use your personal preferences to uncover some new settings or roles that might work for you and stories of nurses who were happy with the moves they made. Before you read more, take a fresh look at your opportunities in direct care.

In this chapter, you'll see three possible ways to approach it.

Choose a Different Point of Care

Look at the delivery of health care along its continuum to get an overview of your options. At one end of the spectrum are hospitals and acute care facilities to handle those who are most sick. But patient stays are shortening, and the number of nurses required there is decreasing. Elsewhere, the need for health care providers will grow as the number of elderly people increases and the interest in wellness and preventative care expands. Community health services will be the prevalent setting for health care and represent the large middle area of the continuum, ranging from extended-care facilities on one end to schools, religious congregations, and even the streets on the other end. Home care represents the last point of care. This area is expected to grow as the number of elderly patients increases, as does the ability to transport medical technology into the home.

Is there a point of care along this continuum that appeals to you? Our personal preferences help lead us. A nurse who can't sit still learns that she thrives in the emergency room. A nurse who likes a slower pace and wants to develop relationships with her patients is happy in a long-term care facility. A nurse who prefers a structured environment opts for the military. Look at this list of some of your setting options. What might work for you?

Hospital/acute care settings

- ☐ Community/suburban
- ☐ Rural
- ☐ University/teaching

Community settings

- ☐ Air and surface transport
- ☐ Ambulatory care clinic
- ☐ Adult day care center
- ☐ Birthing center
- ☐ College or university
- ☐ Community health center
- ☐ Correctional institution
- ☐ Day care center
- ☐ Extended care facility
- ☐ Government/military
- ☐ Health maintenance organization
- ☐ Homeless shelter/mobile crisis unit

- ☐ Long-term care facility/nursing home
- ☐ Medical examiner's office
- ☐ Occupational health services
- ☐ Pain management center
- ☐ Parish/religious congregation
- ☐ Physician- or nurse-managed practice
- ☐ Private or parochial school
- ☐ Psychiatric facility
- ☐ Public school
- ☐ Resort health facility/camp
- ☐ Retirement community center
- ☐ Rural health center
- ☐ State/city/county health department
- ☐ Substance abuse outpatient facility

Home

- ☐ Hospice
- ☐ Other home health agency
- ☐ Visiting nurse service

The enthusiasm expressed by the people I surveyed who had moved into new nursing settings was infectious. They told of how their new work better suited their personalities, skills, or needs. Here are a few of their stories.

Camp Nurse

It did not take Linda E., a Minnesota nurse, very long to decide that hospital nursing was not for her. She wanted to practice professional nursing in a more independent way and not just follow medical directives, as she felt was the case in her local hospital. Her love of the outdoors and her interest in young people led her to take a job in a camp. She's been working full time as a camp nurse ever since. "Once I sunk my teeth into camp nursing," she says, "I've never let go. This is the best nursing practice."

Whereas some camp nurses might work only with a summer program, Linda is the health and safety coordinator for a large, year-round, language immersion camp. In summers, she supervises the health care team that, at times, numbers around 40. During the rest of the year, when there are fewer programs, she alone provides individual health care. However, her responsibilities extend much further. She also manages Occupational Safety and Health Administration (OSHA) programs; negotiates health insurance; monitors three nursing research projects; develops protocols for the camp setting; negotiates out-of-camp provider services; supervises high-risk programs such as archery, fencing, and the ropes course; and functions as the liaison between the program and the American Camping Association. She is a high-energy, professional person who has found a perfect fit.

Linda feels lucky to be able to blend her hobby with her work. She credits her success with "1% inspiration and 99% perspiration." This enterprising nurse recognized a path that was right for her and followed it.

Forensic Nurse

Georgia P., a nurse in Massachusetts, discovered she wasn't suited for hospital work after being on a medical-surgical floor, where the routine failed to provide the kind of challenge she needed. Her next step was to the emergency department, and it was there she saw what she wanted to do—serve as a forensic nurse investigator and sexual assault nurse.

Her career has developed to the point where she educates other people about forensic nursing. She has helped develop a graduate program in this specialty and lectures on the topics of crime scene preservation, evidence collection, forensic photography, and sexual assault nursing to a variety of audiences. Georgia shares these interests with her husband, who is an adult nurse practitioner in an emergency room.

I asked why she decided to revive her nursing career by focusing on forensic nursing. She told me with a laugh that she felt it is a gene she was born with. "You know if you have it," she said. "You watch Columbo and Quincy reruns, read True Crime magazine regularly, and never miss a Patricia Cornwell book."

Another nurse who found this developing specialty exciting is Lynda B., an RN in Washington. She'd worked in cardiac surgery, critical care, and intensive care before starting graduate work in forensic nursing. She chose to work in an emergency department, specializing in sexual assault cases. An intuitive and compassionate person, she feels this is the right specialty for her.

Parish Nurse

Other nurses are working in relatively new nursing settings. Looking for more personal satisfaction in his work, Terrill S., a California nurse, decided on parish nursing. As a parish nurse, he is responsible for health and faith programs within the congregation. His focus is on the health of the whole person—mind, body, and spirit. In his work, he uses the skills he developed as a nurse to make assessments and interventions. He uses interview skills, listens carefully, and gives hands-on care. He tells me his personal faith in God inspired him to make this change. Although some parish nurses are paid for their full-time or part-time work, others voluntarily share their nursing skills and expertise with the congregations of their church or synagogue. A parish nurse might survey a congregation to learn its needs, provide education, arrange speakers, facilitate a support group, do home visits, or provide any number of other services.

Corporate Nurse

Kathleen J. left hospital nursing to work as an occupational health nurse in a major New York banking firm. She took that job because she was curious about the banking industry and wondered how she would fit into a large, competitive company. As an on-site nurse, she found the corporate life appealed to her, and she hoped to use her contacts to secure a job in banking.

She was quite resourceful arranging an interview for an entry-level job at the bank. When a midlevel manager came to the clinic for a routine physical, Kathleen (who has a smile that lets her get away with things like this), told him that she'd return his clothes only after he set up a meeting for her with the manager responsible for hiring trainees. It worked. He got his clothes. She got her job and began a career in banking. For some, changing to a new nursing setting becomes a way to explore work environments other than health care. The promise of a much higher income down the road compensated Kathleen for the low-paying entry-level job she started with.

Many nurses temporarily or permanently choose to do fee-for-service agency nursing for the flexibility it offers and the variety of settings such work entails. They work in hospitals, nursing homes, clinics, rehabilitation centers, and homes. Still others who are looking for diversity opt for more depth in their temporary assignments and become travel nurses. I talked to some nurses who were sold on this option.

Travel Nurse, Full-time

While doing floor nursing in Florida, Sherrill H. noticed that her hospital employed temporary travel nurses because of the fluctuations in the population. Extra staff had to be hired when the Northerners flocked down in winter. She enjoyed listening to these travel nurses' stories. Being young, single, and outgoing, she wanted to see the country, too. So she signed up with one of the largest travel companies and began contracting at hospitals across the United States for 3- to 6-month periods. She's spent time in Texas, California, Pennsylvania, Alaska, and Hawaii. Although this is not a usual perk, Sherrill met her husband, Ed, on an assignment. The two travel nurses were assigned to Alaska the following spring and had a June wedding on Mt. McKinley. She says they love traveling together, and because their housing is paid for by the travel company, they manage to save a lot of their income.

Travel Nurse, Intensive Care Unit

Facing a new environment every few months is not for everyone, but Cathy L., a New York traveling ICU nurse, also loves the lifestyle. She said that being flexible and having a positive attitude are essential for this way of working. In her assignments, she typically has a 2- or 3-day orientation period when she learns the layout of the unit and familiarizes herself with the paperwork. During the last day or two, she observes the work of a "buddy." After that, she feels ready to perform the duties of a staff nurse at that institution. The travel company recruiter often plays an important role in lessening anxiety by learning a nurse's job preferences and matching the nurse with such jobs when they become available.

Travel Nurse, Part-time

Many nurses like traveling part time. A Pennsylvania nurse named Christine S. was looking for a change from her nursing experiences in university and private hospitals. She describes herself as an outgoing, adventurous person who loves seeing new places. Being a lover of the outdoors, she enjoys being a camp nurse during the summer, so travel nursing was a perfect fit. For part of the year she takes on traditional hospital nursing roles in different institutions around the United States, and in the summer, she functions as camp nurse, where she manages an infirmary, does triage, and works with an on-call physician. She loves the flexibility and diversity.

Large numbers of nurses find that making a change in their work setting is the right choice for them, whether it's on a temporary or permanent basis. The energy and involvement that comes with a new environment can be stimulating. Yet changing your setting is only one way to move into a more satisfying job. Nurses who want to stay in nursing have other choices. Take a fresh look from this angle.

Choose a Different Patient Population

Nurses can provide care to people throughout the life span, from birth through childhood, youth, adulthood, old age, to death. As you think about your "People Preferences" in Exercise 7, should you be making a change that will have you delivering care to a different patient population along this continuum? I spoke to some enthusiastic nurses who identified a passion for a certain age group.

Neonatal Nurse

After graduating from a diploma program, Sarah M. worked briefly in a hospital nursery but then signed on as a U.S. Navy nurse and focused on adult care. But when moving to Washington state several years later, she jumped at the chance to work with the very young again at a Children's Hospital and Regional Medical Center, mostly in their intensive care units. Navy nursing had taught her solid organizational skills, she says, but she knew that transient life was not for her. She was right; she's been working at the same facility for almost 30 years.

It's obvious that Sarah is in love with her work. It gives her the opportunity to nurture infants and help them "develop into their own little persons." Her position at the hospital also worked well for her family life over the years because she and her husband did "tag team" parenting by working opposite shifts, never having to use day care facilities for their children.

However, the life of a neonatal nurse can be extremely stressful. In addition to caring for and nurturing newborns, such nurses work with the parents, who often must give up the grand dreams they had for their infants. The neonatal nurse helps parents deal with the stresses of having an extremely immature infant, a child with a lethal genetic disease, a child requiring surgery, or one who is dying. Sarah says that as frustrating as neonatal nursing is, such nurses do see their share of miracles, and that's probably what keeps them at the bedside of the critically ill child.

School Nurse

Roberta H. struggled to find her niche in nursing. When the pediatrics unit of her Maryland hospital underwent a major downsizing, she found herself out of work. That gave her the impetus to make a change. She did temporary work in different environments to try things out, and one day, while substituting for a school nurse, she found exactly what she was looking for. She had such a strong feeling that she belonged in an educational setting, working with young people, that she never looked back.

In the 16 years she's worked in schools, Roberta has moved from junior high to high school, and this older adolescent age group is her favorite. In addition to her regular nursing duties, she teaches classes on health issues, is the advisor of an AIDS awareness club, arranges speakers, and runs support groups.

"They're not coming down for a Band-Aid anymore. School nursing has changed dramatically in the last 8 years," she told me. Roberta has students with seizure disorders, some who have overdosed on drugs, or some who have gone into labor. She says she has really sharpened her listening and assessment skills. "I never know what's coming," she told me. "I like that."

Geriatric Nurse, Retirement Community

Betty D. told me that working with the elderly enriches her life. She began her career in nursing homes and was a staff nurse for two different employers, eventually becoming the director of one of the homes. When she was offered an excellent position as a staff nurse in a drug treatment center, she accepted. Because she loved her work with older people, she assumed she would enjoy nursing in all settings. But the drug treatment center proved to be a frustrating situation for her. The patients, all heavily addicted, had many complicating medical and mental conditions that required immediate attention. The counselors who worked with them at this particular facility were mostly former addicts with training in counseling but no medical training. They were not prepared to identify the other issues, and the nurses were not in a position to make recommendations. It was troubling for her to watch the addicts and their children not getting the help they should be getting. Disheartened, she left after 1 year. It was not a population or setting that worked well for her.

She found a new job with a large retirement community outside of Washington, DC, which returned her to the population she loves, and she is thriving. Betty works with patients from 50 to 103 years of age. At first, the community was strictly residential, with houses, apartments, country clubs, and golf courses, but the residents chose to have a medical facility built in the community. This unit houses six physicians' offices, accommodating about 27 different doctors, two front-desk nurses who handle walk-ins, a 24-hour triage nurse, and medical assistants. As the director of nursing, Betty supervises the program and staff.

I asked why she enjoys this age group. "It comes from within, I guess. I like listening to their wisdom. They love to talk," she says, "with occasional embellishments, I've come to learn, but I find it satisfying to be a social contact for the residents who don't have family or friends nearby." She finds it an uplifting place to work.

I wondered if her patients were sometimes difficult to work with. Betty set me straight. "Yes," she said, "but, usually, it's because they're afraid of missing their tee time."

Hospice Nurse

Suzanne P., a New York woman who had a full life as a wife and mother, says she never really intended to be a nurse. She just loved taking physical science courses and the chance to get out of the house some nights. That's an understandable position for the mother of six boys under the age of 9 years.

Suzanne earned a degree and started out in the medical unit of a psychiatric center. During her time there, she saw many patients in their 90s being resuscitated time and time again, and she became aware of the issue of dying with dignity. She began to read the early works of Elizabeth Kubler-Ross, such as her classic *On Death and Dying*, and developed an interest in serving the needs of terminal patients and their families. At the same time, the hospital tempted her with a "normal job," she says, working full-time Monday through Friday as the trainer. She was responsible for the training of new nurses and the recertification of all medical professionals. The hours were great, but she soon realized something was missing.

Her next nursing job, in acute cardiac care, was too draining, with little time for the counseling she longed to offer the patients and their families. She felt she was without a direction. So Suzanne took charge, assessed her needs and goals, and decided to specialize in hospice nursing. This branch of nursing fit well with her beliefs and nursing style and allowed her to work regular hours so she could also attend to her personal life.

She started as a primary nurse, taking care of patients in their homes, nursing homes, or hospitals then added responsibilities in the hospice admissions process. She takes referrals from physicians, nursing home workers, relatives, neighbors, or anyone with a concern for the patient. Her responsibility is to judge the medical appropriateness of hospice care for these patients. The work is draining but personally satisfying for this woman who gives so much to the dying patients and their families.

She told me how important it is to unwind on weekends. "What do you do?" I asked. "Play stand-up bass in a traveling bluegrass band," she answered.

Still other nurses can bring new life to their work by specializing in an area of practice that requires more advanced education and training. Take a look at this third approach.

Advance in a Special Area of Care

Another way of reviving your career is to develop an expertise in an area of nursing that interests you. There are different ways to go about doing that. One person might complete work required for a bachelor's degree in nursing to receive specialty certification from an agency. Another person might begin a new job in a specialized area and take the additional course work and examination needed for certification. Still another might return to graduate school to get a master's degree and follow the program required for certification as an advanced practice nurse.

Nurses With Specialty Certification

Certification in a specialty area requires a nurse to have an active RN license, experience in that field, the right course work, and a passing grade on an examination based on the scope and standards of practice. Nurses who choose this path find that it identifies them as competent, experienced clinicians and that it also may be taken into account in reimbursement. Most nursing settings have specialization options. The American Nurses Credentialing Center reports on its website (www.nursingworld.org/ancc) that it has certified more than 150,000 nurses in the last 10 years in more than 30 specialty and advanced practice areas.

Specialty areas for which there are significant numbers of certifications include

- ☐ Cardiology
- ☐ Community health
- ☐ Critical care
- ☐ Emergency nursing
- ☐ Gerontology
- ☐ Holistic nursing
- ☐ Hospice and palliative care
- ☐ Inpatient obstetrics
- ☐ Intravenous nursing
- ☐ Medical-surgical nursing

- ☐ Occupational health
- ☐ Oncology
- ☐ Pediatric nursing
- ☐ Rehabilitation nursing
- ☐ School nursing

Observe and question other nurses to explore your options. You can learn more about credentials and educational and experiential requirements from the certification boards listed in Appendix D on page 201 and from the appropriate websites listed in Appendix B on page 189.

Advanced Practice Nurses

Consider one of the four categories of advanced practice nursing if your goal is to go to the top of the clinical nursing field. I spoke with a number of nurses who found career satisfaction by following an appropriate master's degree program, taking the examination, and obtaining this respected certification. Many of their stories also appear in the following chapters because these professionals moved on from patient care and are now teaching, consulting, or running their own businesses. What follows are the stories of some who are still involved in patient care.

Nurse Practitioners

Many nurses today are discovering the pride of providing health care to their own patients in an independent setting or having more responsibility in established settings as a nurse practitioner. They are able to conduct physical examinations, diagnose and treat minor illnesses or injuries, order and interpret laboratory work and x-rays, and in most states prescribe medication. The expanded authority they are given, the possibility of higher reimbursement, the opportunity to focus, and the independence it allows draws many nurses to this option. Nurse practitioners can provide primary health care in many specialty areas, including:

- ☐ Acute care
- ☐ Adult health

- ☐ Emergency care
- ☐ Family care
- ☐ Gerontologic/elder health
- ☐ Neonatal/perinatal care
- ☐ Occupational health
- ☐ Pediatric/child health
- ☐ Psychiatric/mental health
- ☐ School/college health
- ☐ Women's health

I could hear the satisfaction in the voices of the nurse practitioners I spoke with. Here are some of the stories they told me about their work.

Nurse Practitioner, Adult Health

Several years ago, Eileen Z. was disillusioned and frustrated with her work in hospitals. "Everyone's needs were being met but the patients'," this Pennsylvania nurse told me. Her own career path in the hospital offered few appealing choices. In a last ditch effort to save her nursing career, she and a colleague decided to set up their own nursing practice. They began by offering a variety of services, ranging from blood pressure checks to teaching and counseling. These early days showed Eileen and her partner that many people needed the fuller services of a nurse practitioner. She returned to graduate school to gain certification as a nurse practitioner specializing in adult health care. She and another nurse practitioner once again started a private practice. At first their office was open 2 days a week, but the demand for their services was so great they opened it 6 days a week. They see patients in the office or on-site. When called for, they refer patients to other health care professionals. The business is a success and is growing. As she becomes familiar with her clients' needs, Eileen continues to make changes in how she delivers her services.

Nurse Practitioner, Women's Health

Mimi S., a nurse practitioner in Massachusetts, wanted to offer health care in a kinder, gentler setting. She opened a private practice specializing in women's health in a small office that she described as "very homey, with beautiful pictures on the wall, nice wood furnishings, and homemade robes." Like most private practitioners, she wears many hats. She is the main clinician and does the ordering, billing, payroll, supply inventory, hiring, training, marketing, and, as if that isn't enough, during the start-up phase she even washed the robes. Mimi reports that she enjoys the control she has over how and where she provides care to her patients.

Nurse Practitioner, School Health

Sometimes life circumstances dictate a new setting. Carol K., a Connecticut nurse, needed to find a way to balance her work with obligations to her children and husband. Finding that hospital nursing put too many demands on her, she got her post-master's certificate as a family practice nurse practitioner and took a job as an Advanced Practice Registered Nurse (APRN) in a school-based clinic. (Connecticut is one of the states where schools with a large population of low-income students can qualify for on-site clinics.) The clinics are staffed by nurse practitioners who are able to offer a wide range of health care services to the young people they serve. Carol gives physical examinations, teaches health education and pregnancy prevention, and handles acute visits using holistic and prevention models. As you might imagine, each and every day she uses listening skills from her nursing training with this population of teen-agers.

Certified Nurse Midwives

Certified nurse midwives can provide routine gynecologic care to women and offer prenatal, labor and delivery, and postpartum care. Nurses who pursue the certified nurse midwife certification voice strong feelings about a more natural and intervention-free experience for the mother and child and a more holistic approach to women's health care. Nurse midwives can be found working in hospitals, ambulatory care centers, birth centers, and homes.

Nurse Midwife, Independent Practice

It was the promise of new challenges that led Susan W., a certified nurse midwife in Oklahoma, from the hospitals and offices where she worked into private practice. She teamed up with a family nurse practitioner to set up an office and freestanding birth center in their town. In addition to providing childbirth services, these two nurses offer comprehensive prenatal, postpartum, gynecologic, and pediatric health care and are pleased with the independence their practice affords them.

Nurse Midwife, Out-of-Hospital Birth Center

Happy B. settled on full-time work as a midwife at a women's health and birth center in Texas after a long and winding career route. She began her nursing career as a labor and delivery nurse, but as her family moved and grew, she tried different things. At one point, while living in Singapore, she volunteered as a maternal child health practitioner at a Vietnamese refugee camp and saw a very different kind of work. After returning home, she took a position as a "night call" nurse in labor and delivery at a small community hospital, where she found the nursing demanded top clinical skills and critical thinking because the nurses on that shift usually ran the labor and delivery unit alone. It was an important step in her career development.

Family circumstances then forced her take a job with more income, so she became a maternal child health director. As she said, "I at last found a job that could take every single moment of my life and still never be done!." It was too much for even this self-described workaholic, so 20 years after getting her bachelor's degree in nursing, she went back to graduate school to get her master's of science degree in midwifery.

She was part of the first such degree program and reported to me with emotion that they were "subjected to a grueling curriculum of graduate biochemistry, gross anatomy (with all that the term conjures), pathophys, physiology, etc., most of which we took with first year med students. It was nasty, but such a good education. I came out feeling really good, not only about my midwifery skills, but also my academic and practical grasp of primary care."

To support what she refers to as her "midwifery habit," she continues to work a few shifts every month as a labor and delivery nurse.

Certified Registered Nurse Anesthetists

Nurse anesthetists provide care for patients before, during, and after surgery. They may work with an anesthesiologist or work independently delivering anesthetics to patients in a variety of settings. A Pennsylvania nurse explained why she is so committed to this specialty.

Nurse Anesthetist, University Hospital

Margaret told me that when she realized her job as a staff nurse was no longer stimulating to her, she took time to do some soul searching and career exploration. She feels that too many nurses bail out without first trying to "find their niche" within the profession, and she was committed to finding hers. This introspection and information gathering helped her identify anesthetics as the right specialty practice for her. Although the Certified Registered Nurse Anesthetist (CRNA) credentialing program was long and intense, and meant a significant loss of income, the sacrifice was worth it to Margaret during this phase. She says that a large part of her identity and confidence comes from her work, and she is proud of the responsibility and respect she has and the technical skills she uses to care for patients.

Now, as a nurse anesthetist in a university hospital, this high-energy professional thrives on the many challenges of each new day. That's just the way she likes it.

Clinical Nurse Specialists

The role of clinical nurse specialist calls for expertise in a specific practice area of nursing, so nurses gain CNS certification to become the most well-educated clinical nurse. Clinical specialists often are brought in as experts in the nursing process who can troubleshoot, solve problems, and help nurses with collaborative care. The stories of these specialists also appear in the following chapters, which detail how these professionals take on new roles as educators, consultants, researchers, or case managers.

Some of the areas of practice for clinical nurse specialists include

- Adult psychiatric/mental health nursing
- Community health
- Critical care
- Emergency/trauma
- Home health
- Medical-surgical nursing

I spoke to a dedicated nurse from Virginia who told me about the enhanced role she plays as a clinical specialist.

Clinical Specialist, Pediatrics

Ginny G. once weighed the options of nurse practitioner and clinical nurse specialist and determined that the latter was right for her. She saw the nurse practitioner as working primarily with patients following the medical model, whereas she wanted to work with nurses following the nursing model.

She got the required master's degree and certification and began work as a clinical specialist with a focus on pulmonary nursing. She learned an important lesson, she tells me, in those early days. She wanted to teach nurses and patients how to deal with breathlessness, but no matter how important she felt it was, "nobody wanted it." It was then she tuned into the importance of finding a niche—an existing need that others can't or don't want to address. Her work on a hospital committee on nutrition pointed her in the right direction. She now focuses on pediatric nutrition, finding ways to make things better for the nurses and the young patients they treat. The children she works with are unable to eat by mouth for a variety of reasons, including motor impairment, muscular disease, or chemotherapy. As a CNS with physician backup, she sees patients with a defined problem and is given a great deal of freedom in the treatment decision making.

This inspiring nurse says she feels honored to help special needs children. She's stayed with clinical nursing for 30 years because she truly believes it's her mission to help people feel comfortable and supported and offer the best possible care.

I noticed that nurses who stayed in direct care but tried something new felt the same excitement and enthusiasm as those who made more dramatic career moves. For them, patient care proved to be the place they could best use their gifts. Nurses who chose this direction had to first know themselves, then know their options in health care, and finally know how to go about making the change.

If you want to consider other options in patient direct care more carefully, the next few pages will help you get started. Read through the following questions and think carefully about your responses. If your answers are "no" and it doesn't appear right for you, move on. But if you answer any of them positively, read on. Questions such as these will follow each chapter and will help you evaluate the suitability of that career direction for you.

Is This the Right Direction for Me?

- ☐ Am I still committed to providing hands-on nursing care?
- ☐ Would a change in the type of patients I work with revive my enthusiasm for nursing?
- ☐ Do my "People Preferences" from Exercise 7 suggest a different type of patient or facility?
- ☐ Would a change in my work setting increase my satisfaction?
- ☐ Do my responses to "Work Environments" in Exercise 8 or "Wish List" in Exercise 9 suggest a different setting?
- ☐ Is there a nursing specialty I've thought about pursuing?
- ☐ Do my responses to "Areas of Expertise" in Exercise 5 suggest any?
- ☐ Do I need to build my expertise and skills in patient care before making a bigger change?

How Would I Get Started?

- Find nurses who work in the settings that interest you and question them about the positive and negative features of their work. You can ask other nurses or health care workers for names, or you can contact the appropriate professional association to ask them for their contact person in your area. Some association websites have chat rooms or other ways of connecting nurses on-line. The list that follows provides some possibilities.
- If you are interested in specialization, contact the appropriate specialty certification board. A list is included in Appendix B.
- If you need some guidance, speak with a former teacher, manager, or nursing faculty member from a college or university about your options in the field of nursing.

- Consider membership in Sigma Theta Tau International, the Honor Society of Nursing. This is one way a clinical nurse can validate her commitment to the field, make important contacts, and become part of a legacy. For information, write to: Sigma Theta Tau International, 550 West North Street, Indianapolis, IN 46202; telephone, (317) 634-8171; website, www.nursingsociety.org.

Where Can I Get More Information?

There are scores of nursing associations that exist to furnish information, provide educational opportunities, and offer support to nurses interested in their area. Some appropriate to this chapter are listed here. Good on-line links to these organizations can be found at:

www.nursingworld.com
www.nursingcenter.com

See Appendix B for a more extensive list of nursing websites and Appendix D for information on specialty certification.

American Association of Managed Care Nurses
4435 Waterfront Drive, Suite 101
Glen Allen, VA 23060
(804) 747-9698
www.aamcn.org

American Association of Nurse Anesthetists
222 Prospect Avenue
Park Ridge, IL 60068
(847) 692-7050
www.aana.com

American Association of Occupational Health Nurses
50 Lenox Pointe
Atlanta, GA 30324
(404) 262-1162
www.aaohn.org

American College of Nurse-Midwives
818 Connecticut Avenue, Suite 900
Washington, DC 20005
(202) 728-9860
www.acnm.org

American Holistic Nurses Association
Box 2130
Flagstaff, AZ 86003
(800) 278-AHNA
www.ahna.org

American Nurses Association
600 Maryland Avenue SW, Suite 100
Washington, DC 20024
(202) 651-7000
www.ana.org

American Psychiatric Nurses Association
1200 19th Street NW, Suite 300
Washington, DC 20036
(202) 857-1133
www.apna.org

Association of Air Medical Services
110 North Royal, Suite 110
Alexandria, VA 22314
(703) 836-8732
www.aams.org

Association of Camp Nurses
8504 Thorsonveien
Bemidji, MN 56601
(218) 586-2633
www.campnurse.org

Hospice and Palliative Nurses Association
Penn Center West One, Suite 229
Pittsburgh, PA 15276
(412) 787-9301
www.hpna.org

International Association of Forensic Nurses
East Holly Avenue, Box 56
Pitman, NJ 08071
(856) 256-2425
www.forensicnurse.org

International Parish Resource Center
205 West Touhy No. 104
Park Ridge, IL 60068
(800) 556-5368
www.advocatehealth.com

National Association of Clinical Nurse Specialists
3969 Green Street
Harrisburg, PA 17110
(717) 234-6799
www.nacns.org

National Association of Pediatric Nurse Associates and Practitioners
1101 Kings Highway North, No. 206
Cherry Hill, NJ 08034
(609) 667-1773
www.napnap.org

National Association of School Nurses
Lamplighter Lane
PO Box 1300
Scarborough, ME 04070
(207) 883-2117
www.nasn.org

National Association of Traveling Nurses
PO Box 35189
Chicago, IL 60707-0189
(708) 453-0080
www.travelingnurse.org

National Hospice Organization
1901 North Moore Street, Suite 901
Arlington, VA 22209
(703) 243-5900
www.nho.org

National League for Nursing
350 Hudson Street
New York, NY 10014
(212) 989-9393
www.nln.org

National Rehabilitation Association
633 South Washington Street
Alexandria, VA 22314
(703) 836-0850
www.nationalrehab.org

Nurse Practitioner Support Services
212 Railroad Avenue North
Kent, WA 98002
(206) 852-9042

chapter 5

Consider Other Opportunities Within the Domain of Nursing

IN THE LAST CHAPTER, YOU WERE REMINDED HOW MANY OPTIONS YOU HAVE IN patient care. The possible practice settings, the various patient populations, and the specialization areas give you a wide array of choices. Yet even more opportunities open up for someone who wants to stay in nursing but hopes to use her experience in a different way.

There are many reasons a dedicated nurse can feel she's ready to move on to something new. One nurse might want to share her knowledge with less-experienced nurses. Another might want to take what she's learned into the community to help prevent illness. Another might want to help facilities improve their delivery of health care, whereas another might want to be part of ground-breaking medical research. The options we'll focus on now are well suited for an experienced, well-educated nurse who is looking for new challenges within nursing. I found nurses who are sharing their clinical expertise with others in these fields:

- Education
- Consulting
- Research
- Management
- Writing

Education

Nurses are natural teachers. They carefully watch and listen to patients to assess a situation. They're instrumental in helping patients understand their condition and learn how to cooperate with the course of treatment. Nurses often find themselves in the position of explaining developments to the families or reporting their observations and assessments to other medical care givers. Nurses are called upon to anticipate the practical, everyday information the patient will need to care for himself at home and then provide the patient and his family with that information.

This is education at its best—listening carefully, anticipating needs, understanding feelings, respecting them, and sharing information accurately and honestly. No wonder so many nurses who want a different type of experience find that focusing on the education of others is the way to use the skills and knowledge they've gained in patient care. I talked with some enthusiastic, committed nurse educators from different settings about their work.

Nurse Educator, College Level

Many nurse educators are committed to sharing their knowledge with colleagues. These nurses must have a strong clinical background and, depending on the setting, an advanced degree. Some choose to provide continuing education for practicing nurses. Others prefer working with brand new nursing students in an associate degree or bachelor's of science in nursing program. Still others with appropriate experience and educational credentials (often a doctorate) may teach in graduate nursing programs. I spoke to one such nurse about her work.

Pat P. teaches in a pediatric nurse practitioner program in the Washington, DC, area. She says that teaching graduate students satisfies her need for variety. "I tend to get bored fairly easily," she confessed. There is not a lot of classroom time in the nurse practitioner program, so Pat might deliver a lecture only once a week to a class. The rest of the time she is on site visits, monitoring her students' performance, or working at the school-based clinic.

Early in her nursing career, Pat was committed to being a nurse practitioner. She rejected an education emphasis for her master's and focused on the practice of nursing. "The teaching piece of my career was almost accidental," she told me. She was actively recruited as a teacher for the program, and because she is so enthusiastic about being a nurse practitioner, she's a lively and energetic educator. There's one down side of teaching for her—the dreaded Sunday nights. She faces a pile of examinations to be corrected, logs to be checked, abstracts to be reviewed, and sometimes term papers to be read. Will she stay with it, I wondered? "I'm having too much fun right now to leave," she assured me.

Nurse Educator, Staff Development Department

Another option for a nurse who wants to share her knowledge with other nurses is working in the staff development or education department of a hospital. One such nurse is Margy S., an RN in Florida.

After years of working in various hospital nursing positions, Margy began to do occasional teaching and found it better fit her personality and needs at the time. She took a full-time job in a large hospital's department and advanced to director of education and training. She likes the independence and variety in her work. She's responsible for managing the department, doing some of the teaching, coordinating all classes, developing the teaching staff, and promoting her department within the hospital and community. She says her familiarity with nursing requirements, her floor experience, and a master's degree in adult education prepared her for this position.

Nurse Educator, Educational Firm

Angela G., an oncology nurse in California, is doing patient education while she completes her master's degree program. She finds it convenient because she's able to schedule her work around her graduate classes. She explained to me how her current work with patients with cancer came about.

An educational firm servicing pharmaceutical companies hired her for her teaching skills. This firm was commissioned by a drug company to recruit nurse educators to disseminate research information. Currently, she's working on a project involving studies, conducted by nurse researchers at the pharmaceutical company, that gathered information on the effect of exercise and nutrition on fatigue in patients with cancer. The educational company took the results, packaged them as an educational program, and hired independent contractors (such as Angela) to teach the program.

Angela's role is entrepreneurial. She contacts any group or facility she can think of where patients with cancer might be in need of the information she has to share. She works with community agencies, hospitals, physician's offices, outpatient centers, and the American Cancer Society. She teaches classes to patients and their family members, as well as to physicians and nurses. She runs support groups in which patients and family members talk about different issues related to living with cancer. Angela loves teaching and working with patients in this supportive role. However, she misses the one-on-one relationship she had with patients in the hospital, so she would like to combine educating patients with practicing as an oncology nurse practitioner once she gets her degree.

Nurses can establish themselves as independent contractors or work with partners to educate health care professionals, patients or their families, and the general public. There's no limit to the number of topics for which nurses have the expertise that's needed. Here are just a few ideas.

Independent Nurse Educator: Diabetes Education

Beth R., a critical care nurse from Oregon, came up with a new career idea at a continuing education workshop. Her attendance at this diabetes seminar revealed an aspect of health care she found exciting—living well with a chronic illness.

She had begun to feel a divide growing between her work and her beliefs. Beth felt that "care often meant pushing pain killers and relaxants" but strongly believed in promoting a healthy lifestyle through diet, exercise, and stress reduction. She began investigating a more natural response to pain and illness. For the next 3 years, she worked at a diabetes center, where she taught classes to patients with diabetes, held family support groups, and worked with physicians and hospital staff. Her class participants, all from the surrounding area, universally complained about the exorbitant amount of money charged by the pharmacies for the needed prescriptions. She decided to provide discount-priced supplies to people with diabetes in addition to education, support, and information. Her business grew to a point that she was serving a large area west of the Rockies. She attributes her success to the combination of education and low-cost supplies. Beth's business is a shining example of one that sprang from listening carefully to the needs of her clients and helping fill those needs.

Independent Nurse Educator: Childbirth

Sometimes nurses have an intense interest that propels them into the field of teaching. A Florida woman, Sue M., confided to me that she became a nurse for the sole purpose of teaching childbirth education classes. After obtaining her nursing degree, she became certified as a Lamaze technique instructor and has been teaching classes to expectant couples since that point many years ago. Sue works with other nurses who help new mothers with their health and fitness before, during, and after pregnancy. Through this work, Sue became fascinated by the overall health benefits of physical fitness and exercise and decided to share her enthusiasm with others. She became a certified aerobics instructor, and now, in addition to her childbirth preparation classes, she teaches a variety of aerobic exercises and overall fitness to a general population at the community center where she leases space.

Independent Nurse Educator: Parenting

Other nurse educators concern themselves with parents and child *after* birth. After she became a parent, Donna S., a former obstetrics nurse in Maryland who went on to teach in a school of nursing, founded an educational company that presents seminars to new parents. She wanted to address the needs of populations that were sometimes overlooked, so her workshops are directed to both mothers and fathers, single and married people, and natural and adoptive parents. Donna includes health, nutrition, and infant development, as well as family and couple relationships.

Other seminar topics could be developed around a nurse's special interest or expertise. Classes on parenting toddlers, managing special health needs of children, or dealing with sleep issues in young children might find a ready audience. One nurse I spoke to became certified as a parent educator through the Parent Effectiveness Training program (www.gordontraining.com) and offered workshops to parents of both children and teen-agers.

Independent Nurse Educators: Continuing Education Topics

Eileen A., an RN in Florida, taught continuing education classes to nurses for several years before deciding to expand this interest and start a small business offering a number of home study courses to nurses. She created the course list but soon discovered the market told her what she should add or delete. Because of the high level of interest in these subjects, she recently added courses on death and dying, substance abuse, developing quality continuing education, and legal aspects of nursing.

Other nurses, such as Dolores A. from Texas, establish educational consulting businesses addressing other issues of interest to nurses. Dolores enjoys focusing on two professional topics: a general career counseling workshop for nurses, and a workshop that teaches nurses how to set up a consulting business such as hers.

Independent Nurse Educators: Video and Software Production

Another way nurses are educating other nurses is by producing videos, films, and computer software that teach new skills. Linda A., a nurse who now lives in New York, found this to be a great way to combine her nursing experience and her creative energy.

At one time Linda was an IV nurse in an Indiana hospital. While attending a nursing conference, she stumbled on an idea that she parlayed into a successful career. Noticing that a conference presentation was being videotaped, she got the name of the film company from the video technician, called, and offered her services as a consultant for nursing communications. The firm was impressed with her and her idea. She finished getting a master's degree, then moved to New York to become the firm's director of continuing education.

At first her duties included videotaping other fields, but eventually, she focused on and developed the firm's nursing videos. After working with this company for 3 years, Linda set up her own company. She now works closely with nursing associations, creating informational videotapes based on existing courses or books or from original ideas. Linda's work is creative, exciting, and lucrative.

A Missouri nurse with a doctorate and university teaching experience combined new instructional technology and educational materials for nurses. Along with a partner, she runs an educational consulting business specializing in developing interactive software for continuing education course work.

Independent Nurse Educators: Prevention and Wellness

Occupational health nurses generally are hired as care givers to employees of a large organization, but frequently there also is an educational component to their jobs. In many corporate wellness programs, nurses are first responsible for employee screening procedures, where they gather information about an employee's personal medical history, family history, weight, blood pressure, and cardiovascular fitness. Then they may be asked to present workshops to employees on the topics of stress management, weight control, lower back pain, and blood pressure or cholesterol reduction.

However, nurses who are not employed by a company are drawn to teaching wellness or prevention to a general population because it allows them to control the setting, material, and class times.

Some of the wellness topics I found nurses teaching are:

- Aging
- Cardiopulmonary resuscitation
- General fitness and exercise
- Nutrition
- Personal development
- Sexuality
- Sleep
- Smoking cessation
- Stress management
- Substance use and abuse
- Weight control

Independent Nurse Educators: Sexuality

Generally, the wellness classes that are most successful are those that satisfy a need in a community. Some pioneering nurses in California have combined their energies and ideas to form an innovative educational business.

Rona C. and her partner came across many adults in their area who were lacking basic information on human sexuality. They wanted to provide a setting in which people would feel comfortable about expressing their concerns and questions, so they developed a 6-week series of seminars on sexuality that address these needs. They expanded their business to include a component in which they consulted to large employers in their city on the topics of sexuality, the work place needs of pregnant and nursing women, and the establishment of on-site child care programs.

These are only a few stories of nurses who found their niche in education. The nurse educators I spoke to no longer chose to focus on direct patient care but wanted to use their strong human relations, communications, and organizational skills to help others. Each and every one I spoke to felt she was as much of a nurse as ever and was able to help, whether directly or indirectly, a greater number of people.

Consulting

Nurses tell me they're finding that there's a rapidly growing market for their consulting services: in hospitals, health care agencies, institutions, and businesses. In addition to the wealth of theoretical knowledge provided by their nursing education, they also have valuable practical knowledge about everything from systems for patient care to new medical technology.

The basic job of the nurse consultant is to provide the client with expertise that's not available within the client's organization on a short-term or long-term basis. Consultants generally work in one of two ways: they become affiliated with a company or a consulting firm, or they work independently and negotiate their own contracts.

Those with successful consulting practices, affiliated or independent, identify their areas of expertise, put together a package of services to offer, and direct the marketing of those services to institutions, agencies, or individuals who might need their expertise.

People are seeking the advice of nurses on an unlimited number of topics. I found nurses consulting on such things as:

- ☐ Clinical research
- ☐ Compliance with federal and JCAHO regulations
- ☐ Continuing education programming
- ☐ Cost containment
- ☐ Critical care
- ☐ Facilities planning and design
- ☐ Home health care
- ☐ Patient and family education programs
- ☐ Performance improvement
- ☐ Staff development
- ☐ Strategic planning
- ☐ Supplies and equipment

Nurses' consulting businesses have been growing steadily for the last 20 years. Because of budget considerations, hospitals and other smaller facilities must hire outside experts on a contract basis to fill specific needs. This practice, called outsourcing, also has increased because of the growing number of small businesses across the country that must keep their staff small and use outside contractors for services on an as-needed basis.

Consulting comes naturally, according to the many nurses I heard from. They say consulting work follows the familiar pattern of the nursing process. Consultants, too, are called upon to assess a situation, plan an appropriate course of action, and evaluate its effectiveness. Many nurses reported they were drawn to consulting because they felt they had developed such strong assessment and planning skills in patient care.

I heard from nurses around the country who are successfully engaged in consulting activities.

Nurse Consultant, Hospital/Medical Center

Some large hospitals provide their own consultation services, and nurses serve as staff consultants. Karen Z. functions as the director of consultation services for a large urban medical center in Massachusetts. She held a number of positions there, beginning as a staff nurse, becoming head nurse, then assuming the role of staff education director, and finally moving into her current job. With each move she gained valuable experience and an excellent professional reputation. Her department consults on nursing care delivery systems, organizational development, and professional development, primarily in hospitals and visiting nurse associations.

Nurse Consultant, Consulting Firm

Mary K., a Pennsylvania nurse consultant is a partner in a large consulting firm. She explained the essence of the consultant's job from the perspective of a supervisor of other nurse consultants and a practicing one. Mary told me that when handling a strategic planning project, a consultant goes into a hospital, examines the institution's existing programs and services, conducts interviews, gathers data, and reviews the information. She then must determine her recommendations on the basis of her findings and nursing background.

This aspect of consulting is a challenge for many nurses, Mary says, remembering her own early days of uncertainty. Having worked for years in nursing homes, she found that writing her projections and being committed to her recommendations was a difficult task. "Nurses tend to be objective and rely heavily on data. When you move outside [into consulting], you must trust your judgments, even intuition, and not be afraid to come up with predictions." She emphasized that the nurse consultant must learn to have confidence in herself, make effective presentations, and write strong, clear reports, including recommendations. As Mary says, "First and foremost, our 'product' is the written word."

Nurse Consultant, Pharmaceutical Company

Some nurse consultants are employees of a company or health care organization. In the following chapters, you'll read about some whose consulting role primarily is linked to the sales and marketing efforts of their company, but others I spoke to serve more traditional consulting roles for their employers.

Nancy L. of California is employed by a large pharmaceutical company as a link between the company and its products and the physicians and nurses who treat their patients with the drugs. She works primarily with the health care providers on symptom management, but when patients administer their own drugs, as they do with interferon, she consults directly with them, and may meet them at their physician's office or answer their questions on the phone. Nancy also runs support groups for patients and their families. When I asked Nancy if she frequently makes referrals to other professionals, she laughed. "We nurses are the champions of networking," she told me. "We know when something is beyond us, and we find someone else who can help." Nancy often suggests that a patient see a nutritionist or psychologist or whomever she assesses could help the patient with side effects of the medication.

Independent Nurse Consultant: Program Planning

For the most part, nurse consultants are self-employed or work in practices with partners. Some of these nurses focus their consulting businesses on the planning and development of specialized services in their area of expertise.

One such nurse is Michael J., from the state of Washington, who felt, after years of nursing in surgical and emergency room settings in hospitals and providing home health care, that he wanted more independence and variety in his work. Michael founded his own corporation and began consulting on the development of community services, including home health and long-term care, for health care organizations. He told me he is responsible for company policy and procedures, staff recruitment and training, and program development. His master's degree in social work gave him a firm educational base, but he also read numerous books on running a small business and operating a consulting practice to learn how to organize the practice in a professional way and how to sell his services effectively.

Independent Nurse Consultant: Emergency Care

Wenda D.'s experience as an emergency nurse in Vermont and her master's level education gave her the confidence to set up a consulting business with a partner. These two professionals provide help with the development and management of emergency health care delivery systems. Their clients include emergent care clinics, hospitals, nursing homes, and correctional facilities. As is true with many consultants, Wenda and her partner expanded their business by creating and offering continuing education programs for nurses in their specialty.

Self-employed consultants often are involved in getting their message to a larger audience. They do that by writing articles, creating classes, and presenting papers at conferences to gain the respect, exposure, and confidence that help their businesses grow.

Independent Nurse Consultant: Occupational Health

When Corinne S., a nurse in Massachusetts, felt ready for a career change, she looked for a field of nursing that required strong assessment skills. This self-motivated woman describes herself as a creative person who was "ready to break out of the mold." During her years of patient care, she'd enjoyed being able to make nursing assessments quickly and accurately. Her search for the right kind of work led her to consulting. She joined with some partners and set up a consulting business as an occupational health specialist. As a principal in this business, she has responsibilities other than completing projects for her business and institutional clients. She also is responsible for day-to-day management decisions, the initial consultation with clients, continuing education for staff, and the ongoing development of the business.

Independent Nurse Consultant: Mental Health Nursing

Another nurse, Betty N. from Ohio, tells me that her consulting business grew from her interest in sharing her expertise in mental health counseling with other care givers. Because Betty developed a model delivery system for use in post-master's programs in mental health nursing, she often is called upon to speak about it or to consult with facilities that are developing their mental health nursing program. Betty added that she finds it important to continue with patient care while developing her business, so she sees patients part time in her private practice. For her, this is the perfect combination of activities.

Independent Nurse Consultant: Elder Care

Other nurses focus more on patient care. One nurse who chose the independent consulting route is Julie B. of Missouri, who left hospital and clinical work to gain, as she put it, "more independence and control than institutions could offer." She wanted to use the knowledge and experience she'd gained from her years of nursing in a new way, so she and a partner started a consulting business specializing in the care of the elderly. At times she finds herself working on quality control issues with nursing homes; at other times she consults with families who have aging members, teaching them necessary, new skills. Although she was confident about her nursing knowledge, she realized she needed help with certain business functions. Julie praises her local Small Business Administration office for helping her by offering written materials and workshops about setting up a business.

Independent Nurse Consultant: Health Care Administration

Although some nurses with bachelor's degrees develop successful consulting practices, most nurses earn advanced degrees and get additional experience to add to their expertise and credibility when consulting on delivery systems.

One such nurse is Eileen W., a nurse consultant in New York. When she was getting her Ed.D. in health care administration, she took an apprenticeship with an industrial engineering firm. There she learned productivity engineering techniques that the firm used to monitor effectiveness of business operations. Eileen, who sees herself as an objective, systematic thinker, now employs these methods in her work.

She developed a procedure she uses no matter where she's working. First, she determines the practices that are currently in place. Then she analyzes the philosophy of service, the model desired, the quality standards goal; and finally, she recommends what process should be used to deliver services. It is a highly organized procedure, but boiled down to its essence, she is assessing, planning, and evaluating client needs.

Legal Nurse Consultants

Legal work offers nurses tremendous opportunities for those who have strong research skills, excellent communication skills, and an interest in the law. In Chapter 8, you'll read about nurses who became attorneys, but here we'll limit the discussion to nurses who become consultants after short-term paralegal training.

A nurse consultant's tasks might involve reviewing and analyzing medical records, interviewing witnesses, teaching attorneys about the health care aspects of a case, or serving as an expert witness. Legal consultants can work as independent contractors or as employees of law firms, insurance companies, risk management departments, or state agencies. Successful medical-legal consultants generally have clinical experience in a specialty field and often find it important to continue to work in that field in order to be considered an "expert."

Some of the practice areas include:

- Case management
- Criminal law
- Medical malpractice
- Personal injury
- Product liability
- Worker's compensation

Some nurses are involved in general legal advising, whereas others offer more specialized advice.

Legal Nurse Consultant: General

Pamela R., a nurse from Illinois, learned about medical legal consulting and decided to leave her job in a gastroenterology office after 10 years to follow her strong interest in legal issues. Because she had functioned as both nurse and practice manager in her job, she had developed strong organizational and management skills and felt ready to handle her own consulting business. Except for the help she got from the American Association of Legal Nurse Consultants, her training was largely self-directed. She spent many hours networking, studying continuing education tapes, and reading books on consulting and becoming an entrepreneur. Pamela then felt ready to set up a private consulting practice as a legal nurse consultant. Relying on her expertise as a nurse, she works for the law firms that hire her on a contract basis. She reviews medical records; educates attorneys on the nursing or medical issues of a case; stays alert to possible strategies of the other side involving the medical information; performs nursing or medical research; assists with the deposition questions; and locates expert witnesses. She claims that all of her past nursing experience has been helpful and that the attorneys she works for are impressed with her knowledge of medical and nursing issues.

After working in hospitals, community health facilities, and public health settings for years, Sandra E., a nurse from Illinois, set up her own general legal consulting business. Her extensive experience and master's degree in public health gave her the necessary background for legal consulting in such areas as health care administration, gerontology, home health, and community health. During our conversation, she stressed the importance of having the appropriate clinical and educational background for consulting. Attorneys on both sides must accept the nurse consultant's background if she is to give a deposition. Sandra explained her motivation for consulting. "I loved the idea of being my own boss," she admitted. "It was something I *had* to do." She's a person who thrives on diversity in her life, and like all independent consultants, she takes the responsibilities of managing her business, developing new programs, and marketing seriously. "Every single day," she added, "I'm marketing, marketing, marketing."

Legal Nurse Consultant: Medical Malpractice

Lois C., a New York nurse, found a wonderful way to use all of her nursing skills after she received a diagnosis of multiple sclerosis and learned she would need work that was less physically demanding than patient care. To create a new career direction, she thought about the aspects of medicine that interested her most and realized it was the legal and ethical issues that fascinated her. So Lois enrolled in a short-term paralegal course to prepare herself for work as a medical/legal consultant. As she puts it, she now uses her brain, not her body, as she consults with attorneys on medical malpractice. The attorneys rely on her to evaluate medical records for deviations in both medical and nursing practice. It's interesting, fulfilling work for her.

Legal Nurse Consultant: Expert Witness Testimony

Another option for a nurse with a strong interest in the legal aspects of nursing is appearing in court as an expert witness.

Several years ago Laurette A. of New Jersey became involved in an expert witness program sponsored by the state's nurses' association and was referred to attorneys involved in health-related litigation. As an expert witness, she was called upon to research standards of care related to the case and testify in an objective manner about her experience and knowledge of issues involved in the litigation. As she became more involved in the work, she noticed the growing need for nurse experts and began a business as a broker, supplying medical expert witnesses to the legal profession. The contacts she had made over the years helped her to establish this business.

Nurse consultants create satisfying work by knowing their strengths and interests, identifying where their expertise would be valued, and having the confidence to promote this expertise. Many have fashioned custom-made careers—work they look forward to each and every day. I noticed that many of the independent nurse consultants I spoke to were involved in a number of exciting freelance activities. Consulting worked well for them in combination with other professional and personal interests.

They can take pride in the fact that their singular nursing experience and knowledge is in demand and valuable in the marketplace.

Research

Research nurses play a critical role in medical, health, or pharmaceutical research. They are responsible for seeing that all regulatory requirements are met and that the protocol is followed meticulously. Their overriding concern is the patients' safety during the clinical trial.

A doctorate is required for some advanced research work, but most researchers have a bachelor's or master's degree. Nurse researchers can be found in pharmaceutical companies, research organizations, and in teaching and university hospitals. A nurse who explained his work to me is employed in a large, urban research institute in Washington, DC.

Research Nurse

Raj had an educational and vocational background in dairy technology when he came to nursing during a self-described midlife crisis. He pursued an accelerated bachelor's program in nursing and moved into research after 15 months, starting with clinical trials in psychiatry and then in cardiology. His work involves recruiting patients, taking their histories, educating them about the study, disclosing the possible risks and benefits, monitoring lab work and vital signs, and doing the extensive paperwork required in such a highly regulated environment. The studies range from 6 weeks to more than 5 years, with the deciding factor being the time at which the sponsor has sufficient data.

Raj says the work suits him well. A good research nurse, as he describes it, should be an observant, detail-oriented, patient person. On occasion he is involved in 12 trials simultaneously, so he hastened to add that one "has to be able to juggle a lot of hats at one time." He enjoys seeing the patients on a long-term basis and developing relationships with them. A drawback for him is that many of the patients involved in his cardiology trials are extremely sick, and it is hard for him when they die.

This hard-working nurse was clear about the satisfactions of his research work. He says the work gives him a sense of purpose and allows his talents to be used to the fullest extent. Most importantly, he feels he is involved in something that will make a difference.

Management

Nurses who want to develop leadership skills find many ways to grow professionally within their settings. Some become charge nurses or volunteer to be on hospital committees, whereas others take an active role in professional organizations and associations. Many choose to add more responsibility to their clinical work by becoming unit coordinators, nurse directors or nurse managers, generally an option for those with master's degrees. The nurses I spoke to report that, although there is less hierarchy in nursing today, the need for the clinicians to direct nursing activities on the floor will continue.

Nurse Director

Elise O. gave me an account of her work as the nurse director for the intermediate care unit, dialysis unit, wound care services, and hyperbaric services at a hospital corporation outside of Washington, DC. She began by telling me she has 24-hour accountability for these units to emphasize the tremendous responsibility involved in the job. During her time on the floor, she supervises the nurses, interacts with the physicians, handles customer relations, and teams up with the critical care educator, who's the assigned clinical specialist. In addition, Elise is responsible for all staffing matters and adherence to Joint Commission regulations and standards, including implementation of performance improvement projects.

I was curious how a good staff nurse decided to go into management. Elise told me that the appeal of managerial work was the chance to get things done, to have a say in the "big picture" and to work on longer-term projects. The most important qualifications for management, she feels, are the people skills that are required on the job. "It's important that people want to work with you," she told me. "You can learn other aspects of the job, but you have to like working with all kinds of people. If you have high standards for your work, you have to deal with others who may not." Staffing issues rate high on her list of the biggest challenges of the job.

Whereas management is a demanding, full-time option, let's look at another that is frequently a part-time choice.

Writing

Many nurses find that writing is an effective and satisfactory way to share their knowledge, ideas, or research with others. Nurses become involved in writing for the same reasons that people in other fields do. Some write for the sense of accomplishment they feel or for recognition as an expert in a field. Others write to gain credibility or credentials to further a consulting business. Some feel strongly that they want to share their knowledge with other nurses or patients. Others want to inform the public about specialized information they have. Still others see it as a career path and source of income. The reasons nurses take up writing are complex, but their successes are not difficult to understand. Nurses have valuable information and unique perspectives to share with others. A nurse writer who is able to combine the following elements likely will meet with success:

[1.] Expertise in a field of health or health care;

[2.] Knowledge of the needs and interests of her audience;

[3.] Ability to organize material and write clearly; and

[4.] Word processing skills

Nurses' writings appear in textbooks, general interest books, magazines, newspapers, newsletters, and on videos and films. I found out how some nurses who earn money from their writing started out.

Writer, Books

Dianne M. entered writing through the back door. Even while working full time as a labor and delivery nurse, she found the time to do what she loved best—teaching childbirth classes. For 5 years, she happily combined the two jobs. But when the atmosphere began to change in the labor and delivery rooms, Dianne felt the fear of litigation hung too heavily over all procedures, and she decided to leave floor nursing and continue teaching childbirth classes.

When she relocated to Texas, Dianne got a job in a hospital as the family-care coordinator, which involved meeting with expectant couples and introducing them to the facility and an array of childbirth and postpartum courses. She loved this new public relations and education role.

When a prominent obstetrician, who had published a number of books, approached her about collaborating on a book on childbirth, she was thrilled and accepted the offer. But each time she sat down at the typewriter, no words came. Two months later, she had to muster the courage to go back to him and explain that she was not able to write the book. He wouldn't hear of it. With his simple advice, "Just write down exactly what you tell your classes," the words came easily. She filled the book with colorful charts and diagrams and all the helpful things she shared with her classes. At this point, the book has sold more than 70,000 copies!

Dianne feels she's as much a nurse as ever but is now nursing through her classes and written words.

Writers, Magazine Articles

Sue W. and Diana W. are two successful nurse/writers in Kentucky. They wrote their first article together when they noticed that freelance writers who were not health professionals were writing articles on health care issues. They sent around their first article, in which they discussed the rights of patients, and it was accepted by a regional publication. That first success gave them the confidence to continue, and they've since written numerous articles.

Writer, Various Media

Peg J. was a dedicated intensive care and critical care nurse working with cardiac patients in California. A creative and ambitious person, she wanted to do more with her life. Her college major had been journalism, so she began to do some writing. Her now well-established writing career started out with published articles on health-related topics but has blossomed into one in which she writes books, is the editor and founder of a fitness magazine, produces videos, and does television journalism.

Peg credits her nursing skills with her success, and like the other nurse writers, proudly tells me she draws upon her empathy, problem-solving ability, and medical knowledge in her work.

Is This the Right Direction for Me?

For education,

- ☐ Do I have strong verbal skills?
- ☐ Am I a good listener, understanding both the verbal and nonverbal messages of others?
- ☐ Do I have a passion to share what I know?
- ☐ Can I present information in an organized and interesting way?
- ☐ Do I enjoy working with diverse groups of people?

For consulting,

- ☐ Do I have strong verbal and written communication skills?
- ☐ Do I have good observational, assessment, and planning skills?
- ☐ Am I aware of the current issues of health care?
- ☐ Do I have an expertise in an area that currently is of interest to others?
- ☐ Do I like to create or contribute new ideas in my work?
- ☐ Do I enjoy meeting new people and entering new situations?
- ☐ Do I work well without supervision?
- ☐ Am I willing and able to travel?

- ☐ Would I mind working alone a lot of the time?
- ☐ Would I be willing to get out and promote my services to others?
- ☐ Could I manage with an uncertain income?

For research,

- ☐ Do I have strong analytical and observational skills?
- ☐ Am I detail oriented?
- ☐ Would I be willing to do significant amounts of documentation in a timely manner?
- ☐ Would I be prepared for poor outcomes in clinical trials?

For management,

- ☐ Am I comfortable supervising others?
- ☐ Do I like working with a "team" approach?
- ☐ Do I like decision making?
- ☐ Would I be willing to put in extra time when necessary?

For writing,

- ☐ Do I have strong written communication skills?
- ☐ Do I have an expertise in an area that currently is of interest to others?
- ☐ Am I interested in keeping up with new information in my field?
- ☐ Would I enjoy the research involved in writing?
- ☐ Do I enjoy working alone?

How Would I Get Started?

In all areas:

- Stay alert to new developments in nursing and health care.
- Become an expert on your fields of interest:
  - take courses
  - go to workshops and in-services
  - read nursing and general periodicals
  - exchange information with colleagues

- Develop a filing system to collect articles, in-service notes, resource information, etc., in your areas of interest.
- If you intend to be self-employed, use the resources listed on page 130 at the end of Chapter 7.

In education,

- If you would like to teach in a nursing program
  - Meet with a college or university graduate education advisor to learn the requirements for teaching.
  - Contact your local community college or university LPN/LVN or ASN program and inquire about teaching a clinical course.
  - Find a nurse educator who teaches in your specialty area and offer to give one or more guest lectures or develop handouts.
  - Offer to mentor or proctor nursing students at your current work setting.
  - Acquire or hone your computer skills. Schools of nursing often are more interested in faculty who come to them knowing a variety of ways to teach computer use to students.
- Grab any opportunity, inside or outside the work place, you can to teach or demonstrate something to others.
- Get experience:
  - Create and prepare a class or workshop and propose it to the director of an existing continuing education program.
  - Develop a class or workshop and arrange on your own a place to present it. Nurses are sharing their knowledge with the public in such settings as:
    - Assisted living facilities
    - Association conferences
    - Businesses/companies
    - Community groups
    - Health spas
    - Homeless shelters
    - Nursing homes
    - Public health agencies

- Rape crisis centers
- Rehabilitation centers
- Retirement communities
- Schools and colleges
- Voluntary health organizations

The options are limited only by your imagination.

In consulting,

- Identify areas of expertise that could translate into services you might offer. List any that occur to you (look at your responses to Exercise 5 for ideas). Begin by saying, "I will consult on . . ." For example, a person who had extensive training and experience in emergency room nursing and supervision might say, "I will consult on the development of emergency care delivery systems; or the management of an emergency care delivery system; or continuing education programs in emergency care."
- Identify who would need your service. Potential clients could include:
  - Churches
  - Community or government agencies
  - Day care centers
  - Health care professionals
  - Home health agencies
  - Hospitals, nursing homes, rehabilitation facilities
  - Insurance companies
  - Outpatient care facilities
  - Patients and their families
  - Recreational facilities
- Target your marketing to the appropriate individuals, agencies, or institutions when you are ready to begin.
- Develop a consultation contract, using models available from the Small Business Administration services listed on page 130 and those listed in Appendix A on page 188.

Where Can I Get More Information?

American Association for Health Education
1900 Association Drive
Reston, VA 20191
(703) 476-3437
www.aahperd.org

American Association of Diabetes Educators
444 North Michigan Avenue, Suite 1240
Chicago, IL 60611
1-800-338-DMED
www.aadenet.org

American Association of Legal Nurse Consultants
4700 West Lake Avenue
Glenview, IL 60025
(847) 375-4713
www.aalnc.org

American Medical Writers Association
9650 Rockville Pike
Bethesda, MD 20814
(301) 493-0003
www.amwa.org

American Organization of Nurse Executives
One North Franklin, 34th Floor
Chicago, IL 60606
(312) 422-2800

American Public Health Association
1015 15th Street NW
Washington, DC 20005
(202) 789-5600
www.apha.org

American Society for Training and Development
1630 Duke Street
Alexandria, VA 22313
(703) 683-8100
www.astd.org

Association of Clinical Research Professionals
1012 14th Street NW, Suite 807
Washington, DC 20005
(202) 737-8100
www.acrpnet.org

Childbirth Education Foundation
PO Box 5
Richboro, PA 18954
(215) 357-2792

ERIC Clearinghouse on Teaching and Teacher Education
1307 New York Avenue NW, Suite 300
Washington, DC 20005
(800) 822-9229
www.ericsp.org

National Nursing Staff Development Organization
7794 Grow Drive
Pensacola, FL 32514
(850) 474-8762
www.nnsdo.org

Small Business Administration
1-800-U-ASK-SBA (1-800-827-5722)
Regional offices of the SBA appear in Appendix E
www.SBA.gov

Society for Public Health Education
1015 15th Street NW
Washington, DC 20005
(202) 408-9804
www.sophe.org

chapter 6

Practice Alternative or Complementary Care

LET'S MOVE ON TO A TYPE OF PRACTICE THAT HAS ATTRACTED SO MANY NURSES looking for something new that it warranted i ts own chapter.

The roles of alternative care or holistic nurses mirror those we've seen in other chapters. Many continue working in traditional settings and incorporate natural healing techniques into their work with patients in hospitals, offices, nursing homes, or clinics. Some teach the techniques or benefits of a whole body approach to clients or the general public. Others consult on ways to bring alternative care into a work place or health care setting. Still others become independent holistic practitioners. Whatever the setting, providing alternative care offers many nurses the kind of patient contact they find missing in traditional care.

Holistic health care providers consider the whole individual—the body, thoughts, habits, and the environment surround ing the patient. These care givers emphasize the connection of the mind, the body and the spirit. In this chapter, the terms *alternative* and *complementary* are used almost interchangeably, although they each carry a slightly different emphasis. *Alternative* indicates that this type of care takes a different approach than the one of traditional medical care found in hospitals, clinics, and physicians' offices, whereas *complementary* emphasizes that this care can supplement mainstream medicine and does not necessarily replace it.

It is no wonder that nurses are gravitating toward holistic care. The interest in alternative medicine has been growing steadily in this country during the past few decades. Recent studies show that a sizable number of American households contain at least one person who has visited an alternative health care provider. Nurses, as seekers of new ways of improving the lives of their patients, are among the growing numbers of alternative health care practitioners.

Some of the nurses I heard from were self-employed, whereas others were on a payroll. As you've previously heard from the nurse practitioners, self-employment is a perfect option for a self-directed, independent nurse who can live with the risk inherent in running her own business. However, a nurse who wants to practice alternative care as an employee of an existing facility has a lot of exciting options. To determine which setting would be the best for her, she should consider her own interests and needs. She might work in settings such as:

- ☐ Corporate wellness programs
- ☐ Day and destination spas
- ☐ Home health agencies
- ☐ Hospice programs
- ☐ Hospitals, clinics, and nursing homes
- ☐ Hotels, cruise ships, and resorts
- ☐ Pain management centers
- ☐ Physicians' offices

We'll start our exploration of this promising field by looking at holistic practitioners who center their practice on healing or therapeutic touch, then move on to those who provide care through massage and other bodywork. Finally, you'll meet nurses who combine different modalities of complementary care. As you read, you might come across types of care that are new to you, and you'll want a more complete explanation. The associations listed at the end of the chapter will furnish you with descriptive materials, and Appendix A on page 187 lists books that cover all of the techniques mentioned.

Healing or Therapeutic Touch

The principles of healing or therapeutic touch are not new to most nurses. They have been used extensively in hospitals to nurture premature babies and to improve the recovery of surgical and critical care patients. These techniques are meant to comfort and relax the patient, relieve pain, and produce chemical changes in the blood that will lead to self-healing. Using gentle hand motions slightly above the patient's body, the practitioner smooths congestion in the energy field that surrounds the human body. An awareness of the body's energy field is the central concept in these touch therapies and in other modalities discussed in this book, including acupuncture, Reiki, yoga, and reflexology. Much of what we consider holistic or alternative medicine treats the body energy field. Although the concept is new to many in this country, care givers in the Far East have worked with the body's energy field for thousands of years.

I learned much about the benefits of touch therapy from nurses working in different types of settings.

Independent Healing Touch Practitioner

Because the healing touch practitioner hopes to bring about health and self-healing, not only in the physical state, but also in the emotional, mental, and spiritual realms, practitioners find that the relationship between the giver and receiver becomes an important part of the process. Barbara B., a nurse from New Mexico, recognizes this and accordingly has set up her own therapeutic/healing touch practice. She sees patients in their own homes because she finds that her first task is to gain the confidence of the client and create a safe and healing atmosphere. She listens to the client and supports her wherever she is in the healing process. Barbara tells me that she made the change from traditional nursing settings because she felt that hospitals, nursing homes, and other places where medicine is practiced today are places of stress. As she puts it, "today's medical facilities very often do not provide a healing environment for the patient or worker and can even be somewhat toxic."

Healing Touch Practitioner, Holistic Center

Some independent nurses who practice alternative care have joined with others to form holistic care centers. One such nurse is Michaela D., a healing touch practitioner and co-founder of a nonprofit resource center in suburban Washington, DC. This center brings together a group of women who practice different modalities of complementary medicine and offer educational outreach programs. Recognizing the importance of calming surroundings, they have taken great pains to create a physically appealing, relaxing environment, using comfortable seating, fresh flowers, and warm colors. Patients also can enjoy the works of local artists that hang on the center's walls.

Therapeutic Touch, Hospital/Medical Center

Irene M. held a series of responsible nursing positions in Maryland, including one as a supervisor of an obstetrics unit and another as chief nurse of the Reproductive Center of the National Institutes of Health. She now devotes herself fully to teaching maternity nursing in a clinical setting, using therapeutic touch in labor and delivery. Her relaxed communication with patients has always been a great satisfaction to her. She tells me that her compassion, her strong desire to help heal, and the knowledge that she can help others heal themselves led her to focus on the teaching of therapeutic touch.

Reiki Practitioner, Acute Ambulatory Setting

In Massachusetts, Susan D. uses the Japanese energy-based system of Reiki in her work at a large cancer institute. In Reiki, which translates as "universal life energy," the practitioner's hands are gently placed on the patient's body in designated spots on the head, chest, abdomen, and back.

Susan was drawn to this technique, explaining that in the acute ambulatory settings where she had worked, she always felt her strengths were listening and being empathic or understanding others on an emotional level. She studied Reiki and, in a very short time, was able to reach level two, which allowed her to practice Reiki. Because of her personal qualities and her competent use of Reiki, many patients with cancer requested that she continue to help them with this touch therapy, so her health care facility hired her as a patient and family educator.

Susan constantly looks for new ways to add to her ability to help her patients and currently is studying homeopathy, the practice of treating disease by giving patients minute doses of specially selected natural drugs, at a nearby school of homeopathy.

The nurses you've just read about use techniques that don't necessarily involve direct touch, but others are learning techniques that do.

Massage and Other Bodywork

My survey showed that many nurses are practicing techniques that employ hands-on bodywork and manipulation of the muscular structure and soft tissues of the human body. For those interested in this type of work, use the resources listed at the end of this chapter to learn more about such techniques as:

- ☐ Acupressure
- ☐ Ayurveda
- ☐ Craniosacral therapy
- ☐ Myofascial release
- ☐ Neuromuscular therapy
- ☐ Polarity therapy
- ☐ Reflexology
- ☐ Shiatsu
- ☐ Therapeutic massage

Here are a few examples of nurses who chose to treat their patients with a type of hands-on bodywork.

Independent Therapeutic Massage Practitioner

Twenty years ago, Constance P., a Pennsylvania nurse, injured her back lifting a patient. After trying conventional methods of treatment, someone suggested corrective massage. It worked so well for Constance, that she spent the next 3 years studying therapeutic massage so she could practice it independently. She set up a muscle therapy clinic where physicians, hospitals, and rehabilitation facilities send patients to her for soft tissue manipulation. When her patient load became too much for her to handle alone, she had trouble finding other massage therapists with appropriate skills. She began to train them herself and now operates a school where the curriculum is taught by nurses and is designed to meet the special requirements of the nurse massage practitioner. Like many of the open-minded nurses involved in complementary care, Constance is continually learning new modalities. She tells me she currently is studying acupuncture and Chinese herbal medicine.

Independent Therapeutic Massage Practitioner, With Alexander Technique

Karen G., an independent practitioner in Maryland, teaches her clients the Alexander technique and practices massage therapy. The Alexander method helps a person identify and change habits that interfere with natural and efficient coordination. Emphasis is placed on the relationship between the head, neck, and back. Some clients use the technique for improved performance in physical, theatrical, musical, or athletic activities, whereas others use it for rehabilitation and prevention of injuries to the back and neck.

Karen said she made this career move change because, although she enjoyed the stimulation and fast pace of the operating room where she had spent more than 25 years, she felt that quality care was being left out by the emphasis on efficiency—the "time is money" attitude, she says. She made this career move to satisfy her need for more autonomy and control over her work environment. She tells me she had an inner conviction that, although a nursing job is secure and self-employment is risky, this was the right path for her. "It doesn't feel like work," she explained. She truly enjoys the hour she spends with students, exploring their patterns and habits in everyday life and teaching them a technique that helps their bodies function more naturally.

Craniosacral Therapist

Barb C., an Ohio nurse, has been using craniosacral therapy in a private practice she runs from her home. As the mother of two young children, this allows her to work part time around their schedules. She was first introduced to this technique when trying to solve a problem her oldest son had as a newborn. Breast-feeding him was very difficult, she told me, because his mouth and jaw were almost clenched. A nurse at the hospital recommended that she take him to a craniosacral therapist. She was not familiar with this type of work but had always been receptive to natural ways of doing things. (She told me she was once known as the "granola queen.") The therapist treated her son with carefully placed, gentle touches around the head and neck and then with a gloved hand along the roof of the mouth. From that moment on, he never had a problem. Shortly thereafter, Barb took classes and learned the technique. When practicing, she uses a light touch to assist the natural movement of the fluid in the craniosacral system, including the membranes and cerebrospinal fluid that surrounds and protects the brain and spinal cord. Therapists use a pressure that is roughly the weight of a nickel to find the restrictions in the system. Barb was pleased to tell me that often the evaluation itself corrects the problem for her patients, as it did for her young son.

Combining Alternative Modalities

Whereas all of the nurses in this chapter were strong advocates of a holistic approach to healing and were learning new things about holistic health every day, I found some who were trained in and offered a combination of approaches to their patients. Most had begun a practice employing one technique and then added others. Here are a few of their stories.

Chiropractor

Lisa B. knew very little about chiropractic care while she was a practicing nurse in Maryland. She first learned of it through nursing friends who used chiropractors, and when her mother had back problems, Lisa contacted a colleague's doctor to treat her. Lisa went with her mother to the mandatory spinal care class, and this experienced nurse was fascinated. She asked a lot of questions, and after class, the chiropractor commented on her interest and suggested she consider looking into the field. Lisa did and was hooked.

When she decided to leave psychiatric nursing and become a chiropractor, she took on a 5-year program she describes as "very demanding, very intense." She committed herself to this extensive program by putting everything else in her life on hold. Chiropractic care is a natural, holistic therapy, she explained, which takes the nutrition, exercise, sleep, and leisure interests of the patient into account. The chiropractor restores misaligned vertebrae to their proper position through the procedure called "spinal adjustment." In addition to chiropractic manipulations, Lisa sometimes uses the gentle pressure of myofascial release and therapeutic massage to bring relief to her patients. Lisa enjoys being able to spend time with her patients and getting to know them well.

Acupuncturist

Monika R., a Maryland nurse, related that she loves patient care and learning. After years of hospital work, feeling Western medicine was too limiting, she went back to school for an advanced degree in acupuncture to add to her master's degree in clinical social work. This dynamic nurse then became certified as a family nurse practitioner to create the type of practice she wanted.

With acupuncture, she uses needles at key body points to correct energy flow and allow the body to heal itself. Her experience and training make it possible for her to work half time in an acupuncture clinic and the rest of the time in private practice. Monika also uses other treatments to help patients "get in touch with their inner healer," including homeopathy, biofeedback, and psychotherapy supplemented with alternative techniques.

Hypnotherapist

In describing herself, Maureen M., a Virginia nurse, said she's an adventurous person with a low tolerance for hospital nursing. A natural risk taker, she has ventured out on her own providing mind-body psychotherapy with alternative modalities, including hypnosis, guided imagery, aromatherapy, and expressive arts. She also practices healing touch therapy and instructs others in its practice.

To develop the competencies for such an eclectic practice, this energetic nurse has trained and studied for years. She added a 4-year training program at the Colorado Center for Healing Touch and a hypnosis certification program to her solid master's-level education and her psychiatric mental health specialist credential. The practice of hypnosis enables her to guide her patients into a relaxed state that allows them to access other levels of consciousness.

Maureen has designed a work life that excites her. She continues to learn ways of enhancing health and shares them with others.

Homeopathic Practitioners

Louisa S., a Pennsylvania nurse in private practice, emphasized the importance of training and having the right credentials when practicing alternative care. She sometimes uses hypnotherapy when seeing clients but currently is developing her homeopathy practice. As a homeopathic educator, she teaches classes and educates clients on the healing powers of microdoses of natural substances. Louisa stays informed about this aspect of her practice by attending homeopathic study groups.

More information about this field comes from Margaret E., who explained how she became open to alternative medicine. Most of Margaret's early career was in community health nursing, but when she moved to the Washington, DC, metropolitan area, she took a job in biomedical research with the National Institutes of Health, focusing on AIDS. She had heard of therapeutic touch and felt it appropriate to train in it for use with patients with AIDS. Once involved, she went to the American Holistic Nurses Association, where she followed their complete therapeutic touch program, which required that participants become exposed to other alternative modalities. While exploring, Margaret discovered she was most interested in the work of a homeopathic nurse practitioner.

Unlike herbal medicine, which uses crude substances, homeopathic medicine uses highly refined substances in very small quantities. The practice standards were determined by observations of what happened when small amounts of these substances—animal, vegetable, or mineral—were given to healthy people. The substances are intended to stimulate the patient's own healing response. To learn more about this practice, Margaret chose a Canadian program that required 3 years of postgraduate study and an examination at its completion.

Margaret is committed to healing through homeopathy but realizes the practice is not widely understood. She is prepared to spend time teaching her patients and giving workshops to the public to increase their understanding.

Yoga Instructor

Kathleen T. is a Washington, DC, nurse who became interested early in her career in personalizing the contact she had with patients and, as she put it, "keeping people well rather than trying to mend them after their lifestyles made them ill." She has incorporated that philosophy into her work of 25 years teaching yoga to expectant mothers along with more traditional childbirth preparation skills. In addition to this important work, she practices massage therapy and acupuncture. The recent addition of acupuncture to her practice followed a 3.5-year course at a traditional acupuncture center. Kathleen told me her mission also is "to bring another consciousness into our health care system," even though she knows she is educating people one at a time.

The nurses involved in holistic care were an inspiring group. They help their patients by listening to them; learning about them and learning from them; helping them understand and care for their own bodies; and using techniques that bring comfort and improved health. Many nurses turn to this field because it brings them closer to the type of care they were eager to give when they became nurses. More and more nurses are finding it to be a natural step.

Is This the Right Direction for Me?

- ☐ Am I open to going beyond traditional medicine?
- ☐ Do I have a holistic philosophy?
- ☐ Would I like to spend more time with a patient or client?
- ☐ Do I have good listening skills?
- ☐ Do I have a nonjudgmental attitude?
- ☐ Do I have good health and energy?
- ☐ Am I comfortable touching others?

How Would I Get Started?

- Using the resources listed here and other print and on-line sources, read background literature about holistic healing.
- Take short classes from a holistic center or provider to find out where your interests lie.
- Contact associations and accreditation councils for training and accreditation information because accreditation varies widely. The list that follows is a good place to start.
- Think about the settings in which you might like to practice. Are you interested in practicing independently, or would you like to be employed in one of the settings mentioned?
- Talk to practitioners who work in the settings that appeal to you.
- Scout your local natural healing publications and resources. Attend conferences and introductory programs you learn about.

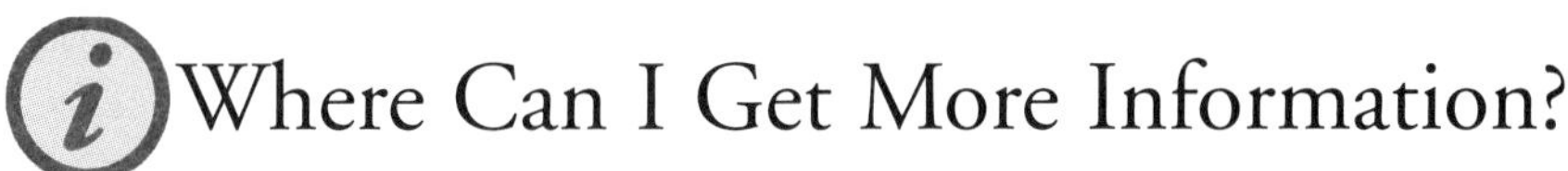

Where Can I Get More Information?

American Holistic Nurses Association
PO Box 2130
Flagstaff, AZ 86003
(800) 278-2462
www.ahna.org

American Center for the Alexander Technique
129 West 67th Street
New York, NY 10023
(212) 799-0468

American Massage Therapy Association
820 Davis Street
Evanston, IL 60201
(708) 864-0123
www.amtamassage.org

American Society of Clinical Hypnosis
130 East Elm Court, Suite 201
Roselle, IL 60172
(708) 297-3317
www.asch.net

Associated Bodywork and Massage Professionals
1271 Sugarbush Drive
Evergreen, CO 80439
1-(800)-458-2267
www.abmp.com

Ayurvedic Institute
11311 Menaul NE
Albuquerque, NM 87112
(505) 291-9698
www.ayurveda.com

Healing Touch International, Inc.
198 Union Boulevard, Suite 202
Lakewood, CO 80228
(303) 989-0581
www.healingtouch.net

International Chiropractors Association
1110 North Glebe Road
Arlington, VA 22201
(703) 528-5000
www.chiropractic.org

International Massage and Somatic Therapies Accreditation Council
28677 Buffalo Park Road
Evergreen, CO 80439
(800) 458-2267

National Association of Nurse Massage Therapists
PO Box 1150
Abita Springs, LA 70420
(888) 462-6686

National Center for Homeopathy
801 North Fairfax Street
Alexandria, VA 22314
(703) 548-7790
www.healthy.net/nch

National Institutes of Health
Alternative Medicine Newsletter
6120 Executive Boulevard, Suite 450
Rockville, MD 20892
(301) 402-2466

Reiki Alliance
PO Box 41
Cataldo, ID 83810
(208) 682-3535
www.reikiseattle.com/tra.htm

section four

Use Your Experience Beyond Clinical Nursing

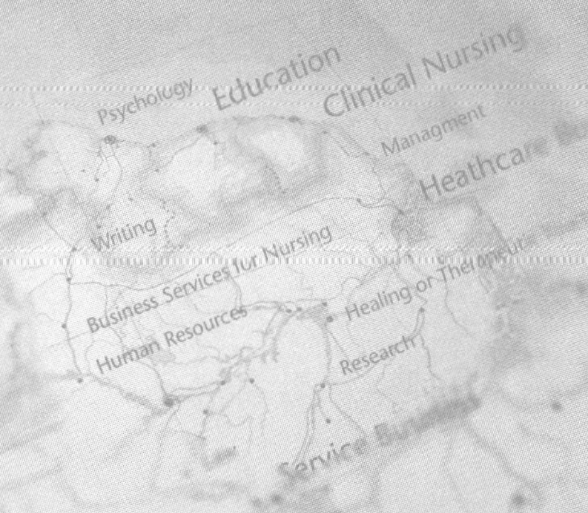

chapter 7

Start a Small Business

THIS WON'T BE THE FIRST MENTION OF NURSES IN BUSINESS.

We've talked about nurse practitioners who focused on a particular population and set up an independent practice delivering health care to them.

We've discussed nurse educators who created packages of course offerings and marketed them on their own.

We've highlighted nurse consultants with confidence in their expertise who created their own companies and independently promoted their services.

We've looked at holistic nurses who provided care and education to their clients.

But there are many more opportunities for self-directed, entrepreneurial nurses who want the many advantages of running their own small business. In this chapter you'll read about a number of them.

The Appeal of a Small Business

In my survey, I asked the nurse entrepreneurs about their reasons for going into business for themselves or into private practice. Certain themes appeared over and over again in their responses.

Independence. "I wanted more independence" was the most frequently mentioned reason for leaving a more traditional setting. Some of the nurses sought freedom from demanding schedules, unrealistic expectations of their workload, or difficult colleagues. Others wanted to be on their own while raising children or preparing for retirement. Most mentioned they knew they generally were happier in a more autonomous setting with less supervision.

Control. This word came up in a variety of contexts. These business owners said they left their former nursing positions because of the lack of control (1) over their time, (2) over the quality of care they were providing, (3) over the nursing decisions being made by others, and (4) over the philosophical direction of health care.

Self-fulfillment. Most respondents said they didn't have a sense of satisfaction about the work they'd been doing in their most recent positions. Some said that something had been lost over the years. They often called this missing piece "self-fulfillment." By setting up their own businesses they were allowing themselves the creativity and personal development they desired. These nurses were eager to create a more challenging situation for themselves, one where they could feel the pride of setting and reaching goals.

Respect. Hand in hand with the notion of more job satisfaction was the idea of a greater sense of professionalism. The nurses I surveyed wanted their nursing performance, education, and experience respected by others. Many who worked in the hospital setting mentioned specifically the lack of respect they felt from physicians or hospital administrators.

The Secret of Success

It was not hard to notice that all of the successful business ventures had one thing in common: the nurse had found a need in the market and filled it. "Find a need and fill it." This should be the mantra for any nurse who wants to run her own business.

In earlier chapters you've seen examples of small business owners who met with success by filling a need. Remember Beth, the diabetes educator in Oregon, whose business grew rapidly after she also began to offer the discounted supplies her clients so badly needed? And Eileen from Florida, whose continuing education business grew as she listened to her clients and added the course work they wanted? Then there was Laurette, the New Jersey nurse who started as an expert witness then went on to form her own brokering business locating expert witnesses.

The other businesses I encountered seemed to fall into one of two categories: they were either directly related to *health care* or they provided a different kind of *service.* Look at these stories for ideas and inspiration.

Health Care Business

Nurses who have worked in home health or specialized care settings sometimes create registries or agencies to supply nurses for those facilities. In a smaller business, the nurse herself might provide the service, but in larger agencies the nurse/owner will focus her time and energy on the management and development of the business.

Home Health Business

Most of us are aware that home care has been the fastest growing segment of the health services industry. In the late 1990s there were about 10,000 home care agencies. By far the majority of these agencies are free-standing, for-profit businesses, and nurses frequently are the owners. Although the overall number of home care agencies fluctuates depending on reimbursement policies, this form of care will continue to be an important part of our health care system.

The nurses I heard from were serious about their responsibility for providing home care services to those who required it because of acute illness, long-term health conditions, permanent disability, or terminal illness.

Home Health Care Provider

Some nurses who recognize a need in their communities for quality home health care have started marketing their *own* professional home nursing services. Michaele B., a nurse in Oregon, promotes her home care as a "reasonable alternative." She explains to prospective clients that it reduces hospital stays, is cost effective, encourages compliance with a physician's recommendation, and produces a positive patient response. She is doing what she loves in the setting of her choice.

Home Health Providers in Partnership

Other nurses join with a partner to offer more complete services. Susan D., a Pennsylvania nurse, continued her work as a head nurse while she and her partner developed their home health business. They worked with their local Small Business Administration office for help with areas that were new to them, such as payroll, billing, and taxes. When the business was fully operational, Susan and her partner took on the managerial tasks, as well as making home visits and scheduling other nurses when the demand was there.

Home Health/Service Business Owner

Still other nurses start small then expand their business as they see additional areas of need. Mary B., a California nurse practitioner who was looking for more control over her work life, first saw that her community needed a home nursing service that offered short-term care. She started a business that offers personalized nursing care, assessment, and advice on a one-time, weekly, or monthly basis. The registered nurses who work for her plan the visits carefully according to the patients' needs. As the business developed, she became aware of other needs and began offering services that go beyond direct medical and nursing care, such as light housekeeping, meal preparation, grocery shopping, and selecting live-in help. This provides a tremendous service to her clients and their families.

Hospice Care Agency Owner

Joyce K., a hospice nurse in New York, told me about her job in hospice care, a growing type of home health agency. Her agency was started by a group of nurses about 25 years ago, as volunteers. Joyce reported that the process of becoming a certified, Medicare-approved New York state hospice program was a long and arduous one for this group of dedicated nurses. Among other things, they were required to show they could provide a full range of medical and support services, could keep careful records, and that there was a documented need for the service in their community. They persevered, and the agency was formed. For years they were the only designated hospice in their geographic area, but Joyce expects to see a rise in the number of smaller hospice and home health agencies, in keeping with the trend toward outpatient care.

Staffing Agency

Some nurse-run agencies offer staffing services along with home health services. These registries serve institutions, agencies, businesses, families, and individuals.

General Staffing Agency Owner

In Pennsylvania, an RN started a successful agency that supplies nurses on a part-time or temporary basis to hospitals and private businesses. Marty M., the founder, was doing agency work as a critical care nurse and going to school to complete pre-med requirements. She saw firsthand the problems that agencies were having with their nurses and clients and felt she could create a better system, a way to keep the nurses more independent, responsible, and better paid. She put her medical career plans on hold and set up her own staffing agency. As a CEO, she finds she works harder than ever, with additional risk and stress, but feels she accomplishes more with less bureaucracy. Marty told me how she "learned by doing" but relied on mentors for support along the way and read books on business for ideas on how to make the business grow. Her work at this point involves running the company, creating new deals, and developing new programs. She is rightfully proud of her contribution.

I asked Marty which personal traits were important to making this change. She described herself as a creative problem solver with "energy and stubbornness." These traits serve an entrepreneur well.

Specialized Staffing Agency Owners

Nurses are finding different ways to structure their staffing agencies. Sandy F., a hard-working nurse in Colorado, heads her own successful firm that supplies critical care nurses to intensive care units and operating rooms for 1- to 3-month stints. She locates, screens, qualifies, and acts as a broker for these specialized nurses. Although her company provides bonuses and other incentives to the nurses, the nurses are paid directly by the employing hospital. Sandy's company receives a finder's fee.

Beverly F., a nurse in California, eased into business ownership. For years she worked as an operating room staff nurse and manager before deciding to leave the hospital setting and join two nurses who had started a business for the temporary staffing of surgical suites. At the time this new idea met with a lot of resistance, but it slowly gained acceptance and the business took off. After a while, she bought out her partners and took over as president, manager, and owner. This forced her to develop new skills in the area of business management. It was tough, but she loved it. This successful nurse explained it to me as many others had: "I'm someone who values my independence above all."

Service Business

Let's move on to an alternative that offers hundreds of possibilities for nurses. This is no exaggeration. Nurses all over the country are starting small service businesses that stem from their interests or observations about what is needed in their community. I learned from the nurses surveyed that there is no limit to the type of service that a business can provide. The important factor for the nurse entrepreneur is a good mix of energy, willingness to learn, and perseverance.

It's not surprising that when nurses set up businesses other than health care, these companies almost always center on a type of service. Nurses have strong people skills that they can use in so many ways. In the following section, you'll read about some nurses who found a need and built a thriving business around it. Their stories will show you how these nurse-run businesses developed.

Personal Training Business Owner

Missy H. didn't intend to have her own business. She had been a cardiology nurse for about 13 years in Ohio before being recruited to serve as a clinical specialist for a cardiac care equipment company. She enjoyed going into the hospitals with the salespeople and demonstrating the use of the equipment in the operating rooms. Reorganization in her company resulted in her taking a sales position that removed her from the clinical setting. She was miserable and left the job without any idea about what to do next.

Urged on by friends, Missy decided to build a personal training business around her love of aerobic exercise. She'd been teaching it part time, always looking forward to the classes, and her reputation as an instructor was growing. She began adding clients slowly, but when she began to specialize, she became as busy as she could be. Missy had found her niche. Her specialty became in-home, personal training with mostly elderly clients having special health needs. Cardiologists, orthopedists, internists, massage therapists, and nutritionists all refer patients to her. Her patients are happy that a cardiac nurse is leading their exercise or strength training program (which usually is prescribed by a physician). For older clients, she is able to offer special attention, such as taking blood pressure and considering their particular cardiac, vision, or balance needs. Prospects are good for Missy and others with an interest in fitness because as the Baby Boom population ages, the need for this service will grow.

Personal Service Business Owner

Claire W., a Virginia nurse, worked for many years in hospitals, primarily in the operating room. She still found time to do volunteer work for her church, and it was through this activity that she stumbled upon a need in her suburban community: people looking for help with short-distance transportation. She decided to try something new and start her own transport service business. The business is small but growing. She usually finds herself helping the elderly get to and from appointments with physicians, although she occasionally serves as a transport service for children whose parents are unavailable.

Claire feels that being a nurse has been a tremendous asset to her business. "People feel comfortable with me," she told me. As far as using her nursing skills, she says she's called upon to listen attentively to her clients, anticipate their needs, and remain calm in the face of a crisis. What a relief the presence of a nurse must be for her clients and their families.

Nanny Agency Owner

Diane S., an RN in Kansas, opened a school for nannies when she saw the need for competent child care workers in her community. With a solid background in pediatrics and four children of her own, Diane easily devised a training program for nannies. After training the workers, she places the young women in homes throughout the country. Like the other service owners, Diane followed our simple rule: find a need and fill it.

Nurses also are capitalizing on the growing need in our country for child care and elder care providers while family members are at work. Nurses are caring for the young or the elderly in their homes, in their clients' homes, or in other sites they lease.

Personal and Business Services to Nurses

In Chapters 5 and 6 you read about nurses who created educational or consulting businesses that focused on providing health care information and advice to other nurses. My research showed that nurses also are coming up with a number of businesses that meet different needs of nurses and are offering these services.

Eileen A., a nurse in Delaware, told me she thought her last job would be running her small health care business. But she was wrong. So many nurses asked her how to set up their own agencies that she began a new business helping nurses with the start-up phase of a business.

Nurses are finding any number of ways to empower their peers by providing them with encouragement, information, and advice.

A nurse in New York became a certified financial planner and now offers financial services to other nurses.

Another nurse, from her New Jersey office, offers image consulting to nurses who want to move into a business setting and present a more professional appearance.

An enterprising California nurse with a heavily visited site on the Internet teaches nurses about the web and the use of computer technology in nursing businesses.

Business ownership is a challenging direction for an energetic, organized and persevering person with an idea. But to get ideas for yourself, first look at this list of some business categories other than health care to see where your interests and skills in communication, organization, assessment, and evaluation might fit.

Business categories:

- ☐ Advertising/promotion
- ☐ Career advising
- ☐ Child care
- ☐ Computer services
- ☐ Consulting
- ☐ Educational
- ☐ Event planning
- ☐ Food preparation
- ☐ Fund raising
- ☐ Home/household service
- ☐ Image consulting
- ☐ Internet
- ☐ Mail order/direct mail
- ☐ Management: time/space
- ☐ Personal service
- ☐ Physical fitness
- ☐ Public speaking
- ☐ Radio/TV
- ☐ Research
- ☐ Word processing
- ☐ Travel

Read through these questions and see if you fit the profile of someone who might successfully run a small business.

Is This the Right Direction for Me?

- ☐ Do I have a viable business idea?
- ☐ Is there an adequate need for the services (or products) I would like to provide?
- ☐ Do I have the financial resources for initial expenses?
- ☐ Do I like to make my own decisions?
- ☐ Am I self-motivated?
- ☐ Am I good at planning?
- ☐ Do I have a high energy level?
- ☐ Do I get discouraged easily?
- ☐ Would I be willing to work long and hard during the start-up period?
- ☐ Am I prepared to make less money than I was making?

How Would I Get Started?

- Define your business idea. Make sure you address these basic issues:
  What service (or product) will you provide?
  To whom will you provide it?
  Where and how will you provide it?
- Check state and local regulations. Nurses often get discouraged thinking about the legal, liability, and insurance issues of starting a business. Although it's true this aspect of a small business requires careful, methodical research, help is readily available and often free. The Small Business Administration frequently was cited as a useful resource.
  Look up your regional office in the list in Appendix E on page 207, check their website (www.SBA.gov), or use the toll-free number that follows to find your district office.
  This office also can refer you to the Small Business Development Center in your area. These centers, which usually are connected with a college or university, offer services and materials on setting up a business. Many local development centers offer free seminars and personalized counseling. They

can direct you to agencies that monitor health care businesses if you're heading in that direction.

Ask them about loans to small businesses and their free or low-cost booklets that flesh out every step you should take.

You also can get advice at no cost from a retired business executive through the Small Business Administration's SCORE program. Several nurse entrepreneurs felt they got the excellent advice on setting up their health care businesses by consulting attorneys who once were nurses. The American Association of Nurse Attorneys (www.taana.org) can provide you with a referral; you call them at (410) 418-4800.

- Using the resources mentioned, develop a business plan. This document will be essential for you and for people you contact about your business.
- List your start-up expenses. You'll want to include such items as:
  - Advertising
  - Computer hardware and software
  - Equipment
  - Insurance
  - Licenses/permits
  - Office supplies
  - Professional fees (lawyer, accountant, consultant, etc.)
  - Salary for yourself or additional staff
  - Space
  - Taxes
  - Telephone system
- Plan for training in business operating procedures. (Many community colleges offer courses or seminars in addition to those offered by the SBA Development Centers.)
- Talk with owners of similar businesses in different locales.
- Learn as much as you can about business considerations. Check the resources in Appendix A on page 187, peruse the offerings at your local bookstore, use the vast resources of the Internet, and visit a college or university library and develop a relationship with a research librarian.

Where Can I Get More Information?

National Association for Home Care
228 7th Street, SE
Washington, DC 20003
(202) 547-7425
www.nahc.org

National Nurses in Business Association, Inc.
56 McArthur Avenue
Staten Island, NY 10312
1-800-331-6534
www.ideanurse.com

Small Business Administration
1-800-U-ASK-SBA
www.SBA.gov
Regional offices appear in Appendix E on page 207.

Some special numbers that may help are:
SBA, Office of Business Initiatives, (202) 205-6665
SBA, Office of Minority Enterprise Development, (202) 205-6533
SBA, Office of Women's Business Ownership, (202) 205-6673
SBA, Office of Veterans Affairs, (202) 205-6773
SBA, Office of Small Business Development Centers, (202) 205-6766

State Board of Nursing for your state. Addresses and phone numbers are included in Appendix C on page 193.

chapter 8

Take Another Professional Direction

WE'VE JUST HEARD FROM NURSES WHO KNEW THEY WERE LOOKING FOR MORE independence and self-direction in their work and were willing to take the risks involved in setting up their own businesses. Now we'll see nurses looking for a professional challenge who are willing to devote years to preparing for a new professional career and deal with the risks inherent in that decision. The fields of medicine, law, and psychology attract numbers of nurses.

Medicine

A nurse educator once told me she was able to spot the students in her classes who would be better placed in medical school than nursing school. They clearly preferred the study of disease and its treatment to learning the nursing process, so she would advise them to make the switch early.

However, sometimes practicing nurses decide they would prefer the role of a physician to that of a nurse. One such person is Ruth C., a pediatrician in Washington state.

Pediatrician

Ruth tells me she always planned to be an Army nurse like her mother and did follow in her footsteps with 3 years of active service after graduating from college with a bachelor's of science in nursing. She became a pediatric nurse practitioner through a military training program and spent 2 years as a nurse practitioner before leaving the service.

Ruth then studied writing and literature, and with her new master's degree in English, taught at a university for 2 years. Not committed enough to pursue the required doctorate, she turned again to nursing but found she would need additional education and training to continue as a practitioner. She felt the part of her previous work she enjoyed the most was the medical decision making and treatment, so at that time she started "the long road to becoming a physician."

She tells me she was attracted by the intellectual challenge of medical studies and the rewards of medical care. "I'd be lying by omission if I didn't include the prestige of the position," she added. She enjoys caring for children from birth into early adolescence and feels she's made a difference in some of the choices her patients make. Medicine, she says, has allowed her to work a part-time schedule and still make a good living.

She emphasized in choosing medicine, one must be committed to the "long haul." She worked 9 years to reach her goal of practicing pediatrics (including 2 years of additional undergraduate work in math and science). Being a physician, she reports, is intense physically and emotionally and tends to strain one's relationships because of the time demands. But it's "a highly rewarding and satisfying career that allows one to continue to grow intellectually and emotionally."

When it came to other professional directions, I noticed two definite paths that nurses are taking: law and psychology. These alternatives offer nurses the opportunity to develop untried skills and acquire a new body of knowledge yet continue to draw upon their nursing experience. So, in this chapter, we'll take our cue from the nurses surveyed and focus on these fields.

Hearing their stories, I began to understand why nurses are drawn to law and psychology. Because of the in-depth personal contact involved, these professions capitalize on a nurse's people skills; they satisfy a nurse's love of helping others; and they offer the possibility of having an even greater and more far-reaching effect on people's lives. No wonder many nurses are willing to make the considerable investment of time, energy, and money required to enter these professions.

Law

As you read the stories of nurse attorneys that follow, you'll notice they share personal qualities that lend themselves to success in the legal profession. Specifically, they are determined, focused, and intelligent people with a strong interest in legal issues. Like those who choose medicine, they must be able to control their circumstances enough to deal with the time, expense, and rigors of a law school education.

Because of the specialized experience and knowledge they bring to their practice, most nurse attorneys represent clients in some way connected to the health care delivery system, such as a patient, a provider, or a hospital. But nurse attorneys also can take on cases that have less medical content involving:

- ☐ Environmental law
- ☐ Family or domestic relations
- ☐ Insurance law
- ☐ Mental health law
- ☐ Personal injury defense
- ☐ Plaintiff personal injury
- ☐ Product liability
- ☐ Worker's compensation

From Nursing to Law

The transition from nurse to attorney requires some alterations in one's thinking for those who have worked in patient care for many years. The American Association of Nurse Attorneys (www.taana.org) addresses some of these adjustments in their booklet *Making the Transition From Nurse to Attorney*. This pamphlet outlines important steps to follow when going from a nursing practice to a legal practice. Included in the list is this advice:

Think Like a Lawyer:

- Talk about the law, not nursing;
- Be confident and assertive;

- Seek out assignments which require legal analysis; do not spend all of your time on nursing tasks such as chart review;
- Think of yourself as a lawyer with a unique background, not as a nurse who has been to law school;
- Put your legal foot forward, but take the nurse with you.

Practice Possibilities

The types of practices available to nurse/attorneys are endless because such individuals are able to incorporate their extensive nursing and medical knowledge into all sorts of settings. Here are but a few examples.

Nurse Attorneys, Specialty Practices

- In Mississippi, a nurse attorney in private practice reviews cases for insurance carriers and advises them on additional medical information that's needed to settle worker's compensation or auto cases.
- A California nurse attorney works for a company that does clinical medical research to help companies get product approval from the Food and Drug Administration.
- A Massachusetts attorney with a nursing background acts as a legal guardian for patients who are mentally incompetent. She handles their affairs, including health care arrangements, financial matters, and housing issues.
- In Georgia, a nurse attorney combines a legal practice specializing in health care law with responsibilities as a teacher in a paralegal program.
- A nurse-anesthetist in South Carolina works as an attorney specializing in disability law. This requires her to synthesize pertinent medical evidence to ensure that it meets federal regulations.
- A nurse attorney in Maryland is employed as the risk manager for a hospital and in that role is required to investigate claims and incidents, teach, counsel, and represent the hospital in negotiations and litigations.

Nurse Attorney, Private Practice: Plaintiff Representation

Sharon C. says she's an independent, goal-oriented, and strong-willed person who was frustrated with what she felt was a lack of respect for her work as a nurse. In response she left hospital nursing, spent several years in law school, then set up a private practice as an attorney in Maryland. She represents people who have experienced serious personal injuries as a result of medical malpractice, defective products, and automobile accidents.

Sharon says she owes her success to her years of nursing and the listening and communication skills, knowledge of anatomy and physiology, and ability to interpret medical records that was required of her on the floors.

Nurse Attorney, Law Firm: Plaintiff Representation

Denise G.'s range of experience as a nurse in an emergency room, postoperative surgical floor, and medical clinic provided a rich background for her new career. This bright, energetic nurse wanted more of a challenge, so she left nursing and decided on a career in law because, as she says, "I'm suited to looking at things analytically."

Every work day, Denise pours through medical records looking for information pertinent to the case at hand. Her ability to do this work so competently won her a job with a Maryland law firm of about 50 attorneys. They recognized this nurse's knowledge of medicine and disease, her understanding of medical terms, and her ability to read and interpret records would prove invaluable to the firm.

In her work as an attorney, she represents plaintiffs in civil suits involving medical malpractice, personal injury, product liability, and worker's compensation.

Nurse Attorney, Law Firm: Medical Malpractice

Diane R., a South Carolina nurse attorney who specializes in working with plaintiffs in medical malpractice cases for her firm, thinks she understands what it is that attracts nurses to the law.

"Nurses are devoted to helping people", she explained, "and that help could be medical or legal." She continued by saying that their knowledge and experience in health care are certainly valuable, but nurses' people skills strongly contribute to their success. To illustrate, Diane described an observation she has made.

"We [nurse attorneys] are much better at mentoring newly graduated lawyers," she said. "We have no problem sharing our time, expertise . . . even forms or software . . . We suspect this is a holdover from nursing and the endless orientation programs and 'return demonstrations' of nursing skills we participated in over the years. Nurses seem to have a skill for teaching at the level of the listener."

Diane's caring way of practicing law has an effect on her clients as well as her colleagues. To illustrate, she regularly receives thank you gifts from her clients, something that is rare for her non-nursing co-workers.

As you've seen, many nurses successfully make the transition to practicing law, and nurse attorneys find many different areas of the law where their expertise is valued. It was obvious from their surveys that all the nurse attorneys were enormously proud of the legal work they perform and of the nursing background that enriches their work. They see their career in law as a way of making a significant contribution to the overall quality of health care.

To learn more about what's involved in the work of a nurse attorney, contact The American Association of Nurse Attorneys, listed at the end of this chapter.

Psychology

As I learned from my respondents, another profession that capitalizes on nurses' strong interpersonal skills is psychology.

It is not unusual for nurses to become interested in their patients' habits, thoughts, and choices. Nurses often feel they would like the opportunity to help people make lifestyle changes that could bring about better health or to spend more time working with the families affected by the illness of a loved one. This leads many to psychology.

Nurses take different routes to the practice of psychology. Some get a master's degree in psychiatric mental health nursing or in marriage and family therapy and become counselors or psychotherapists. Others earn a master's degree in social work, become licensed clinical social workers, and then become therapists. Still others become psychologists by going through the more involved 4- to 7-year program of a doctorate in clinical psychology. Whatever the path taken, the mission is the same: to help clients sort through and understand their issues and take more control of their lives.

Psychotherapists, whether they are psychologists, psychiatric nurses, licensed social workers, or counselors, can practice in a number of environments, including:

- Community mental health centers
- Employee assistance programs
- Group medical practices
- Health maintenance organizations
- Inpatient facilities
- Private practice
- Schools and colleges
- Social service agencies

If you're interested in this field, you'll need to learn more about three issues involved in the study and practice of psychology: accreditation, certification, and licensing. Very briefly,

- An academic program may or may not be accredited by a regional or national accreditation agency, and although the accreditation process is voluntary, most students prefer programs that have this stamp of approval.
- The profession itself may recommend that a national professional review board certify the practitioner, or individual states may require that a professional be certified by a state board.
- A state also may require that a psychotherapist be licensed according to the qualifications determined by their examining board.

You can learn more about these matters from the academic advisor of the graduate school department you're interested in when beginning the application process and from the groups listed at the end of the chapter.

Many nurses I interviewed learned from their patient care experiences the importance of providing mental health services along with physical care.

Family Therapist

Mary Ann S.'s decision to move into a career in psychology also came from her work with critically ill patients and their families. She noticed what she refers to as a "big hole" in the health care system—many patients and their families were not getting counseling when faced with death or the loss of a loved one. So she made the decision to get her doctorate and help people cope with difficult times through counseling.

She now has a thriving family practice where she sees patients from 5 to 95 years old. Yet Mary Ann regrets that her practice has moved away from counseling people who are struggling with an illness or loss. Her ideal job, she explains, would be one in which her therapy sessions would be an integral part of the health care process. To realize that, she says, she would like to be based in a health facility and counsel patients and their families in the clinical setting. She stated she would like to use preoperative and postoperative hypnosis as a way of preparing patients for the trauma of surgery and its recovery and that she would like to guide patients in looking at their lifestyles for factors that contribute to disease.

Although she has not yet found or created such a position, she will work toward that ideal.

Psychotherapist/Consultant

Louise M. started her career in an acute care hospital in Ohio. She became tremendously interested in the psychological issues surrounding critical care situations and, as a result, got a master's degree in mental health nursing. She now provides crisis counseling to individuals and families in her private practice. Because of her expertise, she often is asked to consult on psychological issues related to patient care to health care agencies.

Psychotherapist/Teacher

After getting her doctorate, Gretchen R. worked as a psychologist in a clinic until her finances allowed her to achieve her long-range goal and set up a private practice. Now that she's on her own, this Oregon nurse, in addition to maintaining her private practice, teaches classes and gives lectures. She says these activities are important and serve the dual purpose of providing the exposure that helps her practice grow and giving her balance from the intensity of therapy.

Psychotherapist/Social Welfare Administrator

Marianne B. of Maryland shows us other possibilities for widening the breadth of a career in psychotherapy. This motivated nurse was inspired to become a therapist while finishing her bachelor's degree. When she sampled the specialty fields of nursing, it was clear that psychiatric nursing was the one that attracted her. Because she had been awarded a scholarship for a master's degree, she was able to enter a psychiatric mental health nursing program immediately.

With that degree, Marianne created a career with two components. The major part of her work is a counseling practice at a center where nurses, therapists, and social workers provide a variety of therapy and holistic care services.

The second part of her work revolves around her position as director of wellness at a multilevel program for homeless and formerly homeless women. This program offers a daytime center, night shelter, and a substance abuse treatment program. Her position requires her to create a program that provides information to the women on topics that can help them take charge of their own well-being, such as lectures on menopause and seminars on depression. Under her leadership, the staff and volunteers run groups in which clients discuss problems, learn strategies for change, and get the support they need.

Marianne feels that in both roles, her psychological training allows her to help people in a more holistic way. The work is satisfying to her in part because she has learned to be realistic. Marianne understands that a therapist must be prepared to accept small gains, rather than large gains in the lives of her clients.

As we saw with nurses practicing medicine and law, those who enter the field of psychology add new knowledge and skills to their nursing background to expand the help they give their clients or patients. A nurse who takes one of these three professional directions can look forward to rigorous training, demanding work, the chance to make a difference in someone's life, and an opportunity to be rewarded financially.

Is This the Right Direction for Me?

For medicine,

- ☐ Am I prepared to take a rigorous academic program?
- ☐ Am I prepared to spend the time and money required to complete such a program?
- ☐ Do I have the physical energy for the long and demanding training?

For law,

- ☐ Do I have strong verbal and written communication skills?
- ☐ Am I confident and assertive?
- ☐ Would I be able to handle the amount of study required?
- ☐ Am I competitive?
- ☐ Do I enjoy untangling complex matters?

For psychology,

- ☐ Do I have a high tolerance for individual differences?
- ☐ Can I tolerate long hours of sitting and listening attentively?
- ☐ Would I be frustrated by only small gains made by my patients?

How Would I Get Started?

- Attend meetings of a professional organization or association to learn what are the issues currently under discussion in the field.

- Get to know people working in the field so you can develop a realistic picture of what is involved.
- Go to the appropriate college or university department for help with program requirements, course work descriptions, and certification or licensing issues. Meet with a financial aid officer if needed.

Where Can I Get More Information

American Counseling Association
5999 Stevenson Avenue
Alexandria, VA 22304
(703) 823-9800
www.counseling.org

American Association for Marriage and Family Therapy
1133 15th Street
Washington, DC 20005
(202) 452-0109
www.aamft.org

American Medical Association
515 North State Street
Chicago, IL 60610
(312) 464-5000
www.ama-assn.org

American Psychological Association
750 First Street NE
Washington, DC 20002
(202) 336-5500
www.apa.org

American Psychological Association of Graduate Students
750 First Street NE
Washington, DC 20002
(202) 336-6093
www.apa.org/apags

The American Association of Nurse Attorneys
3525 Ellicott Mills Drive
Ellicott City, MD 21043
(410) 418-4800
www.taana.org

chapter 9

Work on the Business Side of Health Care

TO A NURSE, WORKING ON THE BUSINESS SIDE OF HEALTH CARE MEANS LEAVING one-on-one patient care, but does it mean giving up the satisfaction of helping patients?

I posed this question to a number of nurses who moved into a business role and their answer was a resounding "no." At times, some told me, they missed the daily patient contact, but their new roles allowed them to provide quality care in different ways, sometimes on a scale much larger than before.

Settings for Business-Oriented Nurses

My research showed that nurses move from patient care into a variety of business settings, from a hospital's public relations office to accounting and finance offices. But, just as medicine, law, and psychology lead the professions most often chosen by nurses, certain business areas are of greater interest and have more potential for nurses. These are

- Human resources
- Health care management
- Sales and marketing
- Health association management

It was clear these professionals were still devoted to excellent patient care.

Human Resources

Many nurses get their foot in the corporate door through the human resources department that oversees the "people" side of the organization and includes recruiting, hiring, training, benefits, and career development functions. Here are some stories told by people involved in these interesting careers.

Nurse Recruiter

Mary M., a Pennsylvania nurse found the move from nursing management into nursing recruitment perfect for her. She says she loves going to work now and described her days as screening candidates to fill nursing vacancies, outlining jobs to prospective employees, setting up interviews, and firming up job offers, all within a 35-hour week.

She gets positive feedback from the nursing managers and enjoys immediate satisfaction after successfully filling a vacancy. Her reward is not money, she adds, but a sense that she is in control of her work and has the time to do the best possible job.

Nurse Recruiter, Expanded Role

Grant C. explained how he expanded the role of nurse recruiter in his hospital's human resources department. This Florida nurse headed up a cardiac unit until asked to serve as a temporary liaison between patient services and human resources. Months went by, and he demonstrated exceptional marketing skills and a talent for business assessment and decision making. He created a job for himself by recommending that the patient services group, which includes the nursing staff, have its own recruiter. Now, in addition to posting job openings, writing job descriptions, reviewing applications, and setting up interviews, his job responsibilities include interacting with all levels of management on issues involving strategic planning, marketing, national recruitment and internship programs, and being an active member of several hospital task forces. The down side of the job, he reported, is the long day he must put in, 5 days a week. But Grant clearly enjoys this fast-paced job that places him in the center of the "people" side of hospital management.

Employment Manager

Pam C., another Florida nurse, says her business career began when she recognized and seized an opportunity.

From the beginning of her career, Pam was a committed nurse who thought of her work at a children's hospital as ideal. She started in general pediatrics, moved into newborn nursing, then nursing management. In this last assignment, although the pace was hectic and she was always on call, she enjoyed the challenge. Then her workload grew, and a difficult supervisor came on board, and Pam's job satisfaction plummeted. Around that time she saw an announcement about an opening for a nurse recruiter at her hospital. For the first time she seriously considered a position other than nursing.

Pam reasoned, "I know nursing. I believe in this facility and its values. I can sell it." She applied, landed the job, and began work as a nurse recruiter in the human resources department.

After several successful years, Pam has been promoted to employment manager of the department. This job has expanded dramatically since her hospital became part of a community health alliance, and now she also is responsible for staffing the other health care facilities.

"I'm back on a beeper," she smiled, explaining that she experiences the same hectic pace she once did as a nurse manager, "but I'm filling vacancies with quality people and not making life and death decisions."

Most nurses who have moved into business settings describe occasional ambivalence. Pam described how these "clinical pangs" come every so often, and she asks herself, "What am I doing here?" But she looks at her new work, sees how much it contributes to the overall care of people, and understands, as she says, that for her "nursing has simply grown in another direction."

Director of Human Resources

For Sharon C., it was her course work while earning an master's degree in business administration that opened her eyes to the possibility of incorporating her nursing background into a career in business. When she got her degree, she also took a step in the direction of nurse recruiter. But Sharon didn't stop there.

She is now director of human resources for a large health care alliance in Florida with full responsibility for 7,000 employees. She is in charge of all human resource functions, including recruitment, compensation, benefits, time and attendance, and employee health and safety.

Sharon also organizes special projects such as focus groups to collect employee ideas or an employee opinion survey that involved 17,000 workers. She feels she was prepared for this work by the rigors of her nursing training that taught her critical thinking skills and logic.

This capable nurse is delighted to be combining nursing and business in a way that helps her profession. She admitted, "I owe my success to the fact that I have a true understanding of what happens up there [on the floor] on a 12-hour or 16-hour shift. I've been there. But now I can shape policies . . . even compensation."

Health Care Management

Changes in health care delivery have opened up numerous opportunities in management, and nurses are uniquely qualified to fill them. These new positions involve the evaluation, assessment, or administration of patient care, rather than the practice of it. Nurses are working as quality management, utilization review, case management, and informatics professionals. They work in hospitals or other care facilities, managed care companies, insurance companies, or as private consultants. Here are some of their stories.

Manager, Risk Management Department

Cheryl W. described the day-to-day work of a quality improvement professional and highlighted some of its challenges.

Cheryl was a critical care and emergency nurse in Florida before moving into hospital administration as part of a risk management team. This career opportunity came about in 1985 when hospitals began hiring nurses to assess the appropriateness of care. She describes it as the period when attitudes changed from "the physician is God" to "let's look at the care and hold providers accountable."

When, in the late 1980s, Florida required risk managers to become licensed, Cheryl added this credential through an 18-month licensing process from the Florida Department of Insurance. Although, at the time, hospitals were turning to attorneys and security professionals, Cheryl said that her solid clinical experience and background in quality management put her way ahead. She eventually became the manager of the risk management department, a role that requires Cheryl to wear two hats when evaluating a situation. She puts on her nurse's hat to look at the care, taking into consideration the atmosphere of the floor and the decisions made; then she puts on her risk manager's hat to review the procedures and decisions in a methodical, logical way.

The negative aspects of the job are a challenge for Cheryl, a positive person, who recognizes that people can become angry and defensive when their performance is questioned. She knows the importance of reminding colleagues that punishment is not the goal of the evaluation process.

Her way of evaluating a situation demonstrates her supportive approach to her colleagues. The first question she asks is "What did we do right?" followed by "What was our process?" and then "Was there a kink in the process?" Only after deciding whether the standard of care was met or whether there was a kink in their process, does she determine whether to recommend punitive action.

Another challenging aspect of the work is the volume of problems. When Cheryl is on call, she is inundated with complaints about everything from ants in the cafeteria to toxic odors. She relies on her skill at making assessments and setting priorities to see where to focus her energy in the face of such crises. Otherwise, she is a conscientious person who would want to respond to every request.

Surrounded by negativity, Cheryl says she needs to remind herself of the positive role she plays in her hospital. "I honestly feel that I make a difference," she told me, "that I make things safer for our patients."

Quality Manager, Hospice Program

Heidi V. referred to herself as a "nurse by training," by which she means that she loved what she learned in nursing school but could never see herself performing the duties of a floor nurse. So from the beginning of her career, this New York nurse was looking for alternatives outside of the traditional settings.

The two aspects of care that appealed to her were counseling patients and caring for dying patients and their families. A compassionate person who wanted to see the hospice service available to all dying patients, Heidi volunteered in a local hospice and soon became the salaried director of volunteers. Her nursing training was a tremendous asset, and she quickly built up the volunteer program. As the coordinator, she formulated policies and procedures for this important element of the hospice program and soon added other administrative duties related to the delivery of care.

She is now the quality manager for the program and, like most quality managers I spoke to, she says she is realistically seeking to improve, rather than assure, the quality of the program. The down side of the job for her is the amount of paperwork involved. Not a paper pusher by nature, she knows she must document everything thoroughly. But the compelling positive side for Heidi is the reality of being responsible for changing and improving the way hospice patients and their loved ones are being served.

Nurse Case Manager

Nurse case managers can be found in virtually every health care setting. This relatively new practice area evolved to focus on the cost-effective use of health services and the continuity and quality of care for an individual. Case management generally is directed toward a particular patient population. You can see the variety of practice areas from this list of some special interest groups of the Case Management Society of America.

- Disease management
- Home care
- Managed care
- Military
- Rehabilitation
- Social work
- Subacute
- Worker compensation/occupational health

A busy, independent case manager briefed me on her work. Anne L. first described her work as a case manager in five words: "We cut through red tape." The role has many facets, but an important one is the task of organizing and coordinating resources and services for patients who may not understand the system.

Anne had a long work history in medical-surgical nursing and emergency care before striking out in a new direction. Her first employer was a company that contracted services to hospitals involving risk management and worker's compensation issues. After moving to Florida, Anne got a job with a case management company, for which she focused on the management of catastrophic cases—AIDS, transplants, and spinal injuries. As a per diem employee, she was based at home but performed the work on site.

Now an independent contractor, Anne has a full workload. The process she follows doesn't vary greatly. She meets with the patient, puts together a plan of care, coordinates it with the provider, gets medical approval, talks with the physicians and other health care personnel, helps with the pricing and purchase of equipment, and ensures that the pricing of care and medication is reasonable.

Case management suits her well. For this work, she asserts, you must have an appreciation of quality care, and that requires persistence to ensure that things go well for a patient. She has to "dig, dig, dig" sometimes to find out what's happening in a case and fit together pieces of the puzzle. For someone interested in case management, she points out that the large amount of paperwork required, your accountability to different parties, and the importance of legal issues should be considered. This growing health care field is a promising one for nurses who have a firm grounding in clinical care, knowledge of resources, and experience in a multidisciplinary environment.

Informatics Nurses

More and more nurses are leaving direct patient care and moving into the administration of health and social services as informatics specialists. This blending of nursing science with computer science attracts those with an interest and experience in computers along with a strong clinical background. Informatics nurses collect, process, and manage data that support nursing practice or general health care administration and research. They work in software design, systems management and installation, data analysis, or training, sales, and marketing.

Becky H., an Illinois nurse, told me how she got started. Like most pioneers, she reported, she volunteered for a project. She'd been in mental health nursing for 11 years before she began working with a computerized nursing system in her temporary role as a staffing and registry coordinator. Because of her experience, when the hospital decided to implement an order entry system in the late 1980s, she was offered the opportunity to become the nursing information systems coordinator. She seized it and has been in the specialty ever since.

In her work as a systems analyst, Becky works with teams, assessing user needs, training, and support; concerns herself with information integrity and security; and oversees system development, maintenance, selection, and implementation. She's proud that her work with clinical systems supports clinical processes and makes managing patient information easier and more efficient for nurses.

Becky thinks it's a great time for nurses to consider informatics because of the wide range of opportunities. In addition to the type of job she has, jobs for data managers exist with vendors and health care management companies. She stresses the importance of a clinical background. It's difficult to get the respect of clinical users, she says, if there's no clinical experience. Her advice is simple: Do direct patient care for a while and volunteer for systems projects.

The evolution of her career in informatics took Ruth B. by surprise. "I never thought I'd like machines or computers," she tells me, but she's grown accustomed to them in her rise to senior clinical coordinator with a nonprofit hospital corporation in Maryland.

In the 1980s her hospital instituted its first computer systems for clinical information. The programmers at the time were finance oriented and created programs that simply didn't work. Information services "borrowed" her for a few months for her understanding of clinical functionality. When she returned to the floor, they quickly understood her value, brought her back, and she's been part of information services ever since.

Ruth emphasized that her work now calls for regular contact with people. She's out of her office most of the day teaching, training, or working with nurses and physicians in the acute care facilities. Her position is built on her understanding of the way clinicians do their work and her ability to take that knowledge and incorporate it into software. Ruth feels strongly that her work with system management and software design is important in the delivery of high quality care to the patients.

Sales and Marketing

Companies that supply physicians and hospitals with technical equipment, medical products, and pharmaceuticals have long recognized the benefit of using nurses to market their products and train their customers. Nurses can create instant credibility by speaking to the customers in their own technical language, by quickly assessing the needs of the facility, demonstrating how the product would improve the level of care, and answering questions and addressing concerns. At the same time, many nurses find that sales and marketing also have advantages for them, among them:

- Most nurses already have the relationship, communication, and assessment skills required.
- It is one of the best entries into other corporate positions.
- It usually offers scheduling flexibility.
- It can be financially rewarding.

Very often, people in a sales position are called upon to teach clients about the proper use of the product or consult with them about the implementation of the product. Notice how these sales professionals perform the different functions.

Sales Consultant, Laser Equipment

Valerie S. had experience in pediatrics, medical-surgical nursing, and obstetrics-gynecology before she became the CO_2 laser nurse at a major Georgia hospital. The laser equipment company that supplied the hospital was headquartered in her city, so looking for a new experience, she approached them and asked if they needed a nurse to help train operating room nurses. They liked the idea of a nurse who had used their product to train others, so they hired her. At first unsure of herself, Valerie added to her knowledge of laser physics and safety by reading every article and book she could get her hands on and attending staff training. She soon felt she could field any question posed to her.

Valerie's job consists of doing in-service training for nurses, assisting in surgical procedures, and training surgeons to use the procedures. But "in actuality," she says, "my major tasks and responsibilities are sales, sales, and sales in a two-state district."

Sales Representative, Pharmaceuticals

Paula A. had solid clinical experience as a staff nurse, clinical research nurse, and clinical nurse specialist in oncology in a university teaching hospital in California before she decided to try something new. Avoiding the term "burn out," she told me that she had been taking on more nursing responsibilities and working longer hours. The more efficient she became, it seemed, the more work she was given, and she wasn't good at setting limits. Paula got too attached to her patients, she says, and became stressed. She knew she needed a career change.

Her idea was to create a job for herself at a local pharmaceutical company. Before creating the proposal for the position of oncology nurse educator, she spoke to other nurses who were employed in education and training at pharmaceutical companies, and they helped her shape the job description that she eventually proposed to the nearby firm. Her proposal was accepted, and now she is the sole nurse educator in the company. As a member of the sales division, she creates educational programs and teaches in-service classes to oncology nurses covering her company's products: how to use them, when to use them, and how to manage side effects. Paula has found a helping role that she is better able to manage.

Sales Representative, Intravenous Therapy

A nurse in Connecticut, Debbie S., left cardiac intensive care and recovery room nursing to do marketing and consulting for a home IV therapy company.

Although she originally made the move for a higher salary and better working hours, she quickly learned that she enjoyed sales and marketing. So, this enterprising nurse added a part-time job doing the advertising and marketing for a staffing agency and also demonstrates her love of sales by selling real estate in the remaining hours.

Health Association Management

Associations exist to provide their membership with the most current information about their profession and encourage the exchange of information about problems and solutions. Smaller associations rely heavily on volunteers and part-time help, but larger associations have well-defined positions and offer compensation. My surveys and conversations indicated that nurses are finding their way into management positions in associations that serve all types of medical professionals. Here are some examples.

President, Hospital and Health Systems Association

At various times in her career, Maureen B. has been an army nurse, has worked at a community mental health center, and has been a hospital administrator. Along the way, she got a master's degree in nursing and later a master's degree in business administration with a fellowship at a prestigious business school in Pennsylvania. This intense business training prepared her for her present position as CEO/president of her state's hospital and health systems association. She says she loves the challenge of keeping up with the business, health, and leadership fields. This capable nurse credits her strong work ethic and the desire to keep broadening her horizons with helping her make this successful career move.

Manager, Occupational Health Association

A nurse in Washington, DC, with experience in hospitals, public health, and occupational health found that a move into association management satisfied her need to keep learning and stay challenged. She creates educational tools, including articles, conferences, and competency development programs for people practicing in her association's specialized nursing field. She coordinates a staff of five, performing four separate functions. At all times, she says, she uses the assessment, evaluation, and critical thinking skills developed during her nursing days.

Manager, Specialty Nursing Organization

A Georgia nurse left patient care in hospital and community settings to work in a management position for a specialty nursing organization. In that role, she is responsible for developing and facilitating the continuing education program and practice, as well as coordinating professional development resources for members. She credits the years of following the nursing process with helping her approach everyday challenges with clarity.

Manager, National Hospice Organization

Susan B. described several factors that led to her employment in a management position of a national hospice organization, including her various nursing experiences in hospitals, home care, and hospice care; management positions in and out of nursing; and some favorable professional exposure.

Susan performs several functions in her job in Virginia. On one hand she provides technical assistance to hospice professionals and programs, and on the other, she helps patients and families solve problems around such issues as health benefits.

Like so many nurses I interviewed, Susan says she follows the nursing process each and every day—solving problems, assessing situations, planning strategies, implementing programs, and evaluating results.

Nurses are finding management positions in other types of nonprofit organizations. Appendix B includes resources that will connect you to hundreds of not-for-profit agencies to gather information about employment possibilities.

Human resources, health care management, sales and marketing, and association management are good options for a nurse who is ready to leave patient care but wants to stay in or near that environment and provide a service that benefits those under medical care. The nurses I interviewed feel it's a great way to use other skills, including interpersonal, organizational, sales, and management skills, and still know that they are improving the quality of life for the patients they care about.

Is This the Right Direction for Me?

- ☐ Am I willing to give up clinical nursing?
- ☐ Am I comfortable in a business environment?
- ☐ Can I manage with a cut in salary for an entry-level job?
- ☐ Am I well organized?
- ☐ Do I communicate well verbally and in writing?
- ☐ Can I work with many different personality types?
- ☐ Would I like to work with people at all levels in the organization?

How Would I Get Started?

- Find an appropriate association to join and meet members, read the newsletter, and attend their conferences and workshops.
- Find other nurses who are doing the work that interests you. Consider nurses working in business positions in your current facility or ask friends for names of nurses they know in business or management positions.
- Stop and talk to vendors at the next professional conference you attend to get names of nurses who are working for the company.
- Get as much information as you can about what the job is really like by asking what a typical day is like, what the pros and cons are, what background is helpful, and how a person can enter the field.
- Find out the requirements of the job so you'll be able to address them in a resume or interview.
- Think of ways you might use a volunteer position, an internship, or part-time work to get to know a field and get yourself known.

Where Can I Get More Information?

American Association of Managed Care Nurses
4435 Waterfront Drive, Suite 101
Glen Allen, VA 23060
(804) 747-9698
www.aamcn.org

American Medical Informatics Association
4915 St. Elmo Avenue
Bethesda, MD 20814
(301) 657-1291
www.amia.org

American Nursing Informatics Association
10808 Foothill Boulevard, Suite 160
Rancho Cucamonga, CA 91730
www.ania.org

American Organization of Nurse Executives, American Hospital Association
One North Franklin
Chicago, IL 60606
(312) 422-2800
www.aone.org

American Society for Healthcare Risk Management, American Hospital Association
One North Franklin
Chicago, IL 60606
(312) 422-3980
www.ashrm.org

American Society of Association Executives
1575 I Street NW
Washington, DC 20005
(202) 626-2723
www.asaenet.org

Case Management Society of America
10809 Executive Center Drive, Suite 105
Little Rock, AR 72211
(501) 225-2229
www.cmsa.org

Healthcare Marketing and Communication Council
33 B Route 46 West, Suite B-206
Fairfield, NJ 07004
(201) 575-9555
www.hmc-council.org

Public Relations Society of America
33 Irving Place, 3rd Floor
New York, NY 10003
(212) 995-2230
www.prsa.org

Society for Human Resource Management
606 North Washington Street
Alexandria, VA 22314
(703) 548-3440

section five

Get Started Now: Plan for a Change

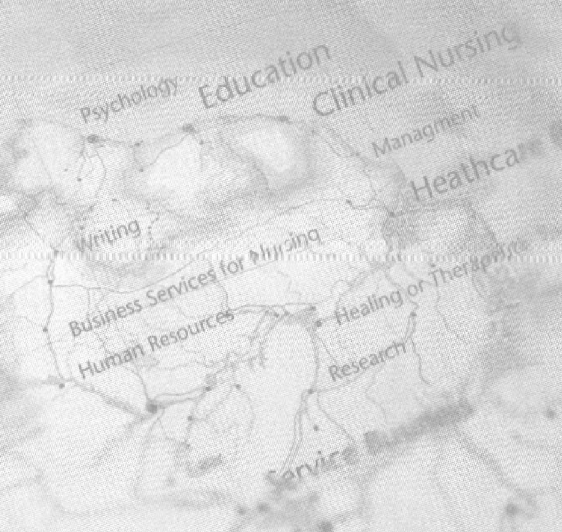

chapter 10

Seven Steps to Take

THIS SECTION IS FILLED WITH IDEAS FOR THOSE WHO WANT TO GET STARTED RIGHT now and will be useful whether you're sure of what you want to do or you only know that you want to do something different. Either way, you'll learn what steps to take to position yourself in a way that will increase your chances of finding more satisfying work and how to stay positive while you're doing it.

Number One: Write Down Your Goals

You might balk at the suggestion of writing down what you want when you're not really sure what that is, but no matter how clear or how hazy your thinking is, it's important (as you'll see) to declare your goals in writing. Some of you probably have already experienced the power of shaping your ideas into one strong written statement of intent. This chapter will help you all do this.

If you're not sure where to begin, look back over your responses to the exercises from the early chapters. What are the most satisfying aspects of your work? What else do you want or need from your work? What type of people would you like to be working with, in what type of environment? Then think about the stories of nurses who have taken different directions. What work appealed to you?

Shaping these elements into goals can help you in three important ways.

- It will point you in a direction.
- It will keep you on the right track.
- It will help you make short-term decisions.

Reaching a goal in the distant future can seem like a daunting task, so it's helpful to be able to look toward your goal and see the steps leading to it. That's what you will be working on now—a long-range goal to point you in the right direction and a series of appropriate short-term goals that you can reach more immediately. Start by shaping a long-range goal.

exercise 10

My Long-Range Goal

Earlier you gave some thought to how you want your life to go, so to begin this exercise, think about what you included in your Summary Statement for Exercise 2. For example, did you value close family ties, gaining knowledge, leadership, spirituality, or some combination of possibilities on the list? In the space provided here or in your journal, write down something that you'd like to accomplish in the future using the time frame of 5 to 10 years. For example, if you'd like to be working part time within 7 years, consider that your long-range goal. Or if you know within 7 years you'd like to be working part time as a consultant, that would be your goal. Or even if you know that within 7 years you'd like to be working part time as a consultant with a small group of partners in a seaside town, that would be your goal. In writing down your goal, be strong and as specific as possible, but no matter how specific or general, it counts as a goal. Using this as a guide, try writing your goal.

Within 5 to 10 years,
I will be working part-time as a consultant on staff development when both kids are in high school.

Within 5 to 10 years, I will

____

____

____

exercise 11

My Mid-Range Goals

Looking at your goal, use the space provided to jot down what actions or experiences can help you get there. You may have ideas about what it might take from the nurses' stories you've just read, or you might first need to follow up some activities suggested at the end of a chapter to see the path more clearly.

For the example used, the ideas might include: *I will need to finish my master's degree, investigate the business aspects of consulting, teach outside the local area, and write about my staff development initiatives.* The mid-range goals would then look something like this:

Within 2 to 5 years:
I will finish my MSN degree program.
I will learn more about the business of consulting.
I will teach continuing education classes in different settings.
I will prepare at least two articles for publication.

Brainstorm your own ideas.
Form these ideas into your mid-range goals.

Within 2 to 5 years

____

____

____

____

exercise 12

My Short-Range Goals

Now, looking at the goals you've listed so far, ask yourself what steps you could take within the next year or two to reach those goals? In the example, you'd think about what you'd need to complete your degree. Then you'd consider how you might learn more about consulting. From the nurses' stories you could see how other nurses learned more about managing a small company or practice. You'd also think about ways you could expand your teaching.

The list might generate short-term goals such as these.

Within the next 2 years

I will take the last three courses toward my MSN.
I will take a workshop on starting up a business.
I will propose a presentation for the annual conference.
I will talk with nurse consultants about their work.

What sorts of actions would you need to take during the next 2 years to realize your short-range goals? Write them down as they come to you.

Form them into actual goals.

Within the next 2 years

____

____

____

____

____

exercise 13

My Immediate Goals

To create your immediate goals, ask yourself what actions are suggested by what you've written? Include things you could accomplish within the next month or so. Continuing with the example provided, the immediate goals, stated as specific, concrete actions might be something like this.

Within the next month

- I will call the local Small Business Administration to get a workshop schedule.
- I will pick up the spring semester graduate schedule.
- I will start a folder on three topics I'm interested in.
- I will contact an association of staff development professionals about membership.

Write your own ideas here.
Make your list of immediate goals.

Within the next month

____

____

____

____

If you want to get started tomorrow, your immediate goals become your "to do" list. You'll have to update this list regularly, but you'll find it easy to do if you have your written goals in a spot where you can review them often.

Goal setting is not a natural activity for all of us, but if you follow these suggestions, you'll have a plan to adhere to, develop, or revise throughout this period of change. Remember, an essential part of this process is putting your goals in writing. You'll find it's an energizing way to begin.

Number Two: Organize Your Personal Information

The goal-setting exercises you've done are meant to clarify, organize, and energize your thinking. Now let's look at information you may be sharing with others.

Begin by Setting Up a Professional Portfolio

Depending on your experience, you'll want to collect materials that create a picture of you as a professional. Include evidence of the education and training you've had, the certifications and licenses you hold, initiatives you've taken, programs you've planned, presentations you've made, research projects you've been involved in, and articles you've written. Add items as you go along.

A person new to nursing may be able to use an accordion file, whereas a seasoned veteran may need a series of folders.

Some of the materials you include might be shared in a future interview, whereas others will be strictly for your personal use. Whatever the case, a portfolio can be a confidence booster and an inspiration for you.

Collect Information for a Written Record of Your Accomplishments

As you've seen in the book, many of the nurses moved into new positions without a traditional job hunt, so it's quite possible you won't have to create a formal résumé. Whatever route you take, you may at some point need to gather together and write down personal information about your goals, education, experience, and skills to give to a person interested in your background. For example, you might want to promote yourself and your plans to a potential practice partner. Or you might need to present yourself to a prospective client or to a banker for a start-up loan or to an editor with an article idea. You've started this process by recording your responses to the exercises in Section 2 so keep them handy for this discussion.

There are a number of items you'll want to include on your personal information sheet or résumé. To get started on a draft of it, record the information to be included under each of these headings.

An Objective

Your *objective* will declare your intent to do a certain type of work, in a certain setting or environment, and possibly using certain skills. This can be a restatement of a long-range or mid-range goal. Some people write a formal objective at the top of their personal information sheet, whereas others prefer to keep it in the forefront of their mind. What matters most is that your objective directs all of the information you include. There is power in focus, and a person demonstrates focus when she says, "This is what I want to do, in this setting, and with these people." The reader will then want to see how your skills, education, and experience support your objective.

If you are ready, try writing your objective.

____

____

____

____

____

Information About Your Education

Remember that your formal *education* is only part of the picture, so look at what you listed in Exercise 5 for other pertinent learning experiences you should include.

First, list your formal education in reverse chronological order, then add other educational experiences that support your objective.

Your Work Experience

Think beyond paid *work experience* when you consider this section. The information you included in Exercises 4 and 5 might suggest other ways to demonstrate your exposure to appropriate experiences. Beginning with the most recent one, list your work experiences in the space provided. Include any peripheral ones such as temporary positions or even significant volunteer responsibilities that are relevant to your objective.

Your Skills

Many people like to write up a résumé or personal information sheet that revolves around their *skills* and experiences, rather than one that lists their formal work experience in chronological order. This type of résumé can work well for people who are making significant career changes or are entering or re-entering a field. No matter whether you organize it functionally (mentioning your skills with specific examples) or chronologically (starting with the most recent experience as you did in the last exercise) or by combining the two, you will want to mention your skills. They are your valuable assets. Don't forget that the interpersonal skills you possess are essential to every work setting, are greatly in demand, and should be included. The results of Exercise 6 will give you a good start.

Which of your skills would you want to include?

Other Professional Accomplishments

Use the space provided to list other items you may want to include. Record your certifications, licenses, honors, and awards you've received and any publications.

Learn About Formal Résumés if You Need to Construct One

The minor style issues of formal résumé writing are vigorously debated among job-hunt professionals, but there are some generally agreed-upon guidelines that I suggest you follow if you need to present a résumé during a job search. For more in-depth information, refer to Appendices A and B on pages 187 and 189.

- Résumés should be a maximum of two pages. If you feel you absolutely *must* include additional relevant material, consider attaching a clear, simple list of items (your presentations, publications, or research).
- The standard formats work the best, not something gimmicky.
- A résumé should be printed on good quality white paper. Use word processing to help you revise and target your résumé to a particular job as well as for easy updating.
- Bulleted lists deliver a lot of information in a readable way.
- Action verbs should be favored over other words in describing work experience.
- Personal information (other than name, address, e-mail address, phone and fax numbers) does not belong. Do not include information on family, marital status, or appearance.
- A résumé should be meticulously proofread.

In a job hunt in the 21st century, it is possible you'll need to transmit your résumé electronically, so consider these several issues.

- E-mail transmission, which is a wonder in many ways, is a disaster for retaining the style of a word-processed résumé included in the body of the e-mail.
- A word-processed résumé sent as an attachment most likely will remain intact.
- An organization may ask you to use a "résumé builder" for standardization of personal information. The work you've been doing in this chapter will be your guide in completing it.
- If you're given a choice in submitting your information, decide if your own format would be a better tool for promoting yourself than the standard one they use.

Think of this written product, whether it's a personal information sheet or a formal résumé, as your first important promotional tool. Give yourself a head start by organizing the information now.

Number Three: Practice Promoting Yourself

Creating a written document promoting yourself is only part of the picture. You'll also need to talk about yourself in a positive, self-promoting way if you're making any type of career change. Even if you don't mount an all-out job campaign and a series of interviews isn't likely, prepare yourself to talk to others. You might have to talk to the admissions officer of a graduate program you'd like to enter, to a supervisor about adding responsibilities to your job, or possibly, to potential customers or clients for the business or practice you've started.

If you're uncomfortable about this prospect, start small. Practice talking about yourself, your ideas, and your plans to trusted friends. You can hear how you sound and get some feedback. Add colleagues or acquaintances you feel comfortable with. But when you are ready to work on a more professional presentation, here are two important pieces of advice for you.

Learn to toot your own horn. Most of us are uncomfortable when we're in a position to tell someone how good we are, and during this transition you might find yourself in a situation where you'll need to do just that. Even if you naturally tend toward modesty, you can learn to talk comfortably about your strengths. Try phrasing things this way to help you express yourself more easily:

I've been told that I

____

____

____

Supervisors have commented on my

____

____

____

My evaluations say that I

____

____

____

My colleagues tell me that

____

____

____

I have a reputation for being

____

____

____

I've been recognized for

This second bit of advice will also help you promote yourself.

Prepare five stories. This is the single best preparation you can make if you're faced with a formal interview. The exercise provided will allow you to assume a more active role in the interview, rather than simply answer the questions posed to you. Use the space provided to get ready if you have a certain job situation in mind.

Here's how to start. Ask yourself, well before the interview, the critical questions:

"What qualities should a person in this position have?"

"Which of my personal qualities do I want to emphasize?"

When you've answered these questions and identified these traits, come up with situations in your past in which you demonstrated these very qualities. Pick five in which the actions you took, the decisions you made, or the program you developed turned out well. Answer these three questions about each of your five situations:

What was the problem (or situation) at the time?

What steps did I take to remedy (or improve) it?

How did it turn out?

Situation 1

Problem/situation

Steps taken

Outcome

Situation 2

Problem/situation

Steps taken

Outcome

Situation 3

Problem/situation

Steps taken

Outcome

Situation 4

Problem/situation

Steps taken

Outcome

Situation 5

Problem/situation

Steps taken

Outcome

____

____

____

____

Once you've prepared what you'd like to say about these situations, trim your stories to the bare bones. Practice saying them wherever you're comfortable—in the car, to a friend, or in the mirror. They'll come to you easily at the right moment if you practice them, and you'll be more confident and articulate and have a more impressive interview.

As you can see, you're not going to be *telling* them "I have such great leadership skills." You're going to be *showing* them through your stories. Stay alert in the interview for the right time to elaborate on an answer with a story. You can probably use them as examples when answering some of the standard interview questions such as, *"Why should we hire you? What do you see as your strengths? What did you like or dislike about your last job? Do you work well under pressure?"*

This is something you can start thinking about today.

Number Four: Rally Support Around You

You'll feel a lot better through this period of change if you have people who share your ups and downs. However, some of your friends, colleagues, and family members may not be the best people to help you work through your new plans or listen to your ideas. They might have their own reasons for wanting you to stay right where you are.

One nurse found that the nurses on the night shift with her were the best people to talk with about her ideas. They were all at different points in their lives, and they enjoyed listening to each other sort through their different career issues.

Another nurse found a ready-made support group when she went to her first meeting of the American Holistic Nurses Association. There she found a wonderful group of like-minded colleagues who shared information and ideas with her and really listened to her.

Another nurse, who wanted to begin a consulting business, hired an enthusiastic business coach who encouraged her along the way, helped her clarify her thinking, and added a professional touch to the marketing of services she planned to offer.

Which colleagues, friends, or family members are most supportive of your change?

____

____

____

____

Do you know other people who have recently made career changes who might be helpful to you?

____

____

____

____

Which organizations or associations could you contact?

____

____

____

____

Whether you have ready-made support in your circle of friends, colleagues, and family or whether you have to go out and seek it, make sure you're not going through this alone.

Number Five: Meet New People

During a career transition period, people you meet can be a source of energy, ideas, and even leads for you, so it's a good time to get to know new people. It may seem like an added burden to a busy schedule, but try to fit in some type of initiative. You can meet others by taking a continuing education class, volunteering, attending social organization and club meetings, or through professional associations. One nurse in the midst of a career change who wanted to develop her public speaking skills joined Toastmasters International (www.toastmasters.org), a group that provided her with a platform, some role models, and a ready-made support group.

If you have a specific career interest, there's a direct way of meeting people who can help you with your plans. That way, which often is referred to as *informational interviewing*, involves contacting people who are doing what you would like to be doing and asking them for information about their work or their field.

To dispel any pressure you might feel about making a contact, you may need to remind yourself that you're only asking them for 15 minutes of their time and not a job. You're trying to learn whether or not you would be interested in their line of work. Occasionally a mutual interest begins at an informational interview, but that's not the purpose and shouldn't be counted on.

A lot of people get stuck on the very first step—finding people to contact. I once had a class do an exercise to prove how resourceful they could be in finding contacts. At one class session, I brought in current newspapers that contained some kind of business news—the local business journal, a weekly business supplement, and some business sections of the daily newspaper. I challenged the students to find four or five leads they could follow up from a quick look at the paper. One woman in the class who was interested in the tourism industry found four announcements in that week's newspapers and followed up the next week.

She noticed:

- the name of a woman who had been promoted to manager of tour and travel sales for a major golf resort;

- the name of a woman who had been named regional director of marketing and sales for the five area hotels of a major chain;
- the time and place of the monthly meeting of the local chapter of an association of saleswomen; and
- an educational workshop being offered by Meeting Planners International.

She found that people being promoted to responsible positions in organizations often are highlighted in business or professional news, and it's a great source of leads because they're usually enthusiastic about their promotions and may be willing to help someone who's interested in their work.

The Internet gives you another avenue for making contacts. (However, resist the urge to make this your only networking tool. Face-to-face contact has its benefits.) Because of its reach, the Internet is unrivaled in its ability to connect people who can help one another or share information. To make use of this alternative, think about your affiliations, including colleges, universities, associations, organizations, and professional fraternities. Their websites may have bulletin boards or chat rooms where you can seek out others with whom you have a ready-made bond.

List possible sources for your leads. Include newspapers, magazines, nursing journals, Internet sites, and organizations. Ask family and friends for more ideas.

____

____

____

____

____

A Virginia nurse made good use of the informational interview. She was trying to establish herself as a consultant with an expertise in staff team building, an area she became interested in while working as the community relations director for a home health agency. This resourceful nurse met with directors of various agencies and institutions to find out what their most pressing staff issues were. She was not ready to take on clients at that point but hoped to tailor her offerings as a consultant to the needs of such organizations. She would say to these administrators, "This is what I am thinking of doing. Does it make sense? Would you put resources behind something like this?" This research helped her define the work that she wanted to do and introduced her to directors who might someday need her services.

Number Six: Follow Your Interests

Keep doing what you love to do. For some of you this may be stating the obvious, but for others it may serve as an important reminder. It is too easy during a time period when you are focused on work issues to put aside other things in your life that have been important. Your interests can keep you centered, positive, and sometimes even lead you in an unexpected direction.

For example, if you enjoy the outdoors and camping, schedule it. Remember Linda E., the nurse from Minnesota, who loved the outdoors and worked herself into a position as the health and safety coordinator of a large year-round camp. If you like reading murder mysteries, make time for them. You may remember Georgia P., from Massachusetts, who did additional graduate work and parlayed this interest into a successful career in forensic nursing. If you love taking or teaching aerobics, keep it up. Missy H. built a thriving personal training business in Ohio from her passion for exercise. As some of our featured nurses found out, you never know where your interests will lead you.

This brings to mind the story of Yvonne K., a nurse from Oregon, who shared photos of the wonderful sculptures and colored pencil drawings she does of animals. She started years ago and tried out different art media, developing her talent as an artist throughout her nursing career. While living and working in Tennessee, she displayed her art in the Tennessee Nurses Associations first art show and showed her work in two hospital staff exhibitions.

Over the years, Yvonne's art work has appeared numerous shows, been published in artists magazines, appeared in books on technique, and been purchased for private collections from California to New York. All of this was accomplished while

Yvonne worked as a nurse. When her health recently forced her to retire from nursing, she had a fully developed second career waiting for her.

Which of your interests do you want to make time for no matter how busy things get?

____

____

____

Whether it's for enjoyment, improved mental health, or part of a bigger plan for the future, it's important to stay involved with the things you enjoy. Through this involvement you can:

- Stay positive and confident
- Meet new people
- Learn new things
- Discover new career possibilities
- Create part-time or retirement options

At the very least, staying involved with things you enjoy will lead to a fuller, more interesting life.

Number 7: Stay Light on Your Feet

This last step is less concrete than the others but equally as important. It doesn't negate the importance of setting your goals and objectives but asks you to remember that as you move along your intended path, your actions may uncover some unintended, but welcome, opportunities. Like a basketball coach who might direct a player, "Stay light on your feet," remind yourself regularly to stay alert to things around you that present themselves as you move ahead in the direction you've chosen.

The following story illustrates how things can evolve if you're open to unexpected opportunities that arise. Please note the passages in bold print highlight Joanne's actions, during the pursuit of her goals, that allow for what may at first seem like luck.

Ten years ago, Joanne L. was employed as a critical care nurse in a Florida hospital and felt she was perfectly suited for life in the emergency room. **She loved patient care and worked energetically to do the best possible job.** When her quality work was recognized and she was promoted to supervisor, **she was well on her way to realizing the goal she had of becoming a director of nursing.**

At that time, the hospital was looking for a computer system to put in place. **Joanne was interested in how this would affect the delivery of care in the emergency room, so she asked a lot of questions.** When it came time for a representative to sit on a fact-finding committee, the director of nursing, who'd noticed Joanne's interest, asked her to be part of the committee. So Joanne went to the meeting where representatives from all departments of the hospital met with the computer experts. **She wanted to be clear about how this new system was going to affect the clinicians, so she asked question after question.** She wanted to make sure this would actually improve patient service, making it better as well as faster.

The hospital administration went with the computer system and then needed a systems analyst with a clinical background to help put it in place. When a friend suggested to Joanne that she apply, she laughed because she knew absolutely nothing about computers. But her name was put forward, and she was offered the job. When she pleaded ignorance about the high tech world, they assured her it didn't matter. **She had demonstrated she really knew how the hospital worked.** So she accepted the position.

Joanne quickly became an important part of the project team, **making recommendations from the perspective of a long-time nurse.** After **she took some short-term, background classes in computers and learned hands-on about programming from the team,** the work became even more interesting to her.

"This would really help!" became her battle cry as **she pointed out how the computer could help them do things more quickly and easily.** The system improvements that Joanne recommended added revenue to the hospital, and the administrators were noticing. **Joanne was making herself more and more valuable.**

Over the years, her hospital became part of a larger entity, a community health alliance, and Joanne was named the director of clinical systems and director of information services for the entire organization. As an administrator explained it to her, she had gotten the job because they were looking for someone with focus who could move them to the next level. It was clear to everyone that **Joanne never lost her focus: providing the best possible patient care.**

Joanne's story contains a few reminders about the importance of staying open and ready to move in an unexpected direction.

- Change, however unsettling, also can create opportunities.
- Being observant and curious sets you apart from many others.
- Learning something new can open doors.
- New jobs are being formed every day, so keep your eyes open.

No matter how far along you are in the career change process, there are steps you could be taking now.

Review the advice in the seven recommendations you've just read and decide where to begin. Even your smallest acts will move you toward more satisfying work and a better state of mind. Remember:

- Be clear about what you want.
- Be prepared to show other people what you have to offer.
- Talk yourself up.
- Meet new people.
- Surround yourself with supportive friends.
- Keep up with your interests.
- Stay alert for new possibilities that arise.

A Final Reminder

Whatever you do, remind yourself daily that you, as a nurse, have so much to offer and so many alternatives. The skills you've developed, the experience you've gained, and the knowledge you've gathered contribute to the number of possibilities open to you. If you'd like to share your pride, take the opportunity to tell others, especially young people, about the profession. Let a young neighbor or cousin know what's possible with a nursing degree. Talk with the children or teen-agers who watch you care for relatives. Take advantage of the opportunity to appear at a high school career day or talk to your child's class about nursing.

You may choose to make a slight change or a dramatic one. Perhaps something you've learned about yourself in the exercises will suggest an adjustment you could make in your current situation that will make it more satisfying. Perhaps taking on a different responsibility will spark a new enthusiasm for your work. You might choose to stay in patient care but work in a different setting or a more specialized one. You may find an advanced nursing practice is the right move for you or a practice using a method of alternative care. Perhaps you'll share your nursing knowledge and experience with others through teaching or consulting. Or you might discover that you'd like to help patients in a broader way in a legal or business setting.

By going through this book, you've demonstrated that you'd like to make it an informed and personal choice. Be excited and proud of all of your options. Enjoy the process of sorting through them and creating a work life that's right for you.

appendix A

Resources

Reference Books

Consultants and consulting organizations directory (21st ed.). (2000). Detroit, MI: Gale Group.

Encyclopedia of associations. (2001). Detroit, MI: Gale Research Inc.

Encyclopedia of medical organizations and agencies. (2000). Detroit, MI: Gale Research Inc.

Feuerman, F., & Handel, M. J. (1997). *Alternative medicine resource guide.* Lanham, MD: Medical Library Association, Scarecrow Press.

Job seeker's guide to private and public companies. (1994). Detroit, MI: Gale Research.

Medical and health information directory. (1998). Detroit, MI: Gale Research Inc.

Plunkett, J. W. *Plunkett's health care industry almanac.* (2001). Plunkett Research, Ltd.

Standard and Poor's register of corporations, directors and executives. (2001). New York: Standard and Poor's Corporation, annual.

Career/Education Books

Bolles, R. N. (1999). *Job-hunting on the Internet.* Berkeley, CA: Ten Speed Press.

Bolles, R. N. (2001). *What color is your parachute?* Berkeley, CA: Ten Speed Press.

Bozell, J. (1999). *Anatomy of a job search: A nurse's guide to finding and landing the job you want.* Springhouse, PA: Springhouse Corporation.

College and university almanac 2001: A compact guide to higher education. (2000). Princeton, NJ: Peterson's Guides.

Nursing programs 2002: Peterson's guide to nursing programs. (2001). Princeton, NJ: Peterson's Guides.

Official guide to graduate nursing schools. (2000). New York: National League for Nursing.

Official guide to undergraduate nursing schools. (2000). New York: National League for Nursing.

Scholarships and loans for nursing education. (1997). New York: National League for Nursing Press.

Sher, B. (1995). *I could do anything if I only knew what it was.* New York: Dell Trade Paperbacks.

The AJN career guide. (2001). New York: American Journal of Nursing Co. (This can be viewed on-line at http://www.nursingcenter.com/career/ajn.cfm.)

Tieger, P. D., & Barron-Tieger, B. (2001). *Do what you are: discovering the perfect career for you through the secrets of personality type.* Boston: Little, Brown and Company.

Weddle, P. (2000). *Cliffs notes: Finding a job on the Web.* Foster City, CA: IDG Books Worldwide Inc.

Special Interest Books

Covello, J. A. (1998). *Your first business plan: A simple question and answer format designed to help you write your own plan.* Naperville, IL: Sourcebooks, Inc.

Holm, K. C. (ed.). (2001). *Writer's market: 8000 editors who buy what you write.* Cincinnati, OH: Writer's Digest Books.

Huff, P. (1998). *101 best small businesses for women.* Rocklin, CA: Prima Publishing.

Jones, R. (1998). *Educational and career opportunities in alternative medicine.* Rocklin, CA: Prima Health, 1998.

Kishel, G., & Kishel, P. (1996). *How to start and run a successful consulting business.* New York: John Wiley & Sons, Inc.

Law School Admissions Council, Inc. (1998). *A practical guide to law as a career: So you want to be a lawyer.* New York: Broadway Books.

Lyons, D. J. B. (1997). *Planning your career in alternative medicine.* Garden City Park, NY: Avery Publishing Group.

O'Hara, P. D. (1998). *SBA loans: A step-by-step guide.* New York: John Wiley & Sons, Inc.

Perkins-Reed, M. (1996). *Thriving in transition: Effective living in times of change.* New York: Touchstone Books.

Powell, S. K. (1999). *Case management: A practical guide to success in managed care.* Philadelphia: Lippincott Williams & Wilkins.

Root, H., & Koenig, S. (1998). *The small business start-up guide.* Naperville, IL: Sourcebooks, Inc.

Shenson, H., & Nicholas, T. (1997). *The complete guide to consulting success.* Chicago: Dearborn Financial Publishing.

Sherman, A. J. (1997). *The complete guide to running and growing your business.* New York: Times Business.

Stillerman, E. (1996). *The encyclopedia of bodywork: From acupressure to zone therapy.* New York: Facts on File.

Vallano, A. (1999). *Careers in nursing: Manage your future in the changing world of healthcare.* New York: Kaplan Books.

Vogel, G. (1994). *Entrepreneuring: A nurse's guide to starting a business.* New York: National League for Nursing Press.

If you'd like to order a book directly from the publisher at their website, you can locate it on-line at www.lights.com/publisher.

Or you can use a search engine such as those on page 191 to find it.

You can also order through one of the on-line booksellers:

www.amazon.com

www.bn.com

www.borders.com

appendix B

Internet Resources

Websites for Nurses

These websites are a good place to start for information on continuing education, job openings, resume posting, association links, nursing specialties and chat rooms where nurses can share information:

www.nursesportal.com
www.allnurses.com
www.nursingcenter.com
www.nursingspectrum.com
www.rnweb.com

The official site of the American Nurses' Association also has detailed information about credentialing:

www.nursingworld.org

For information and a link to state nursing associations:

www.nursingworld.org/snaaddr.htm

Special interest sites

www.nursingindex.com (Canadian nurses)
www.pna-america.org (nurses from the Philippines)
www.nahnhq.org (National Association of Hispanic Nurses)
www.nbna (National Black Nurses Association)
www.aamn.org (American Assembly for Men in Nursing)

Career Websites

There are literally hundreds of websites for someone interested in career development to visit, but these are a few good sites to begin with.

For additional personal assessment exercises:

www.personalitytype.com
http://web.missouri.edu/~cppcwww/holland.shtml

For educational and financial aid information:

www.petersons.com
www.gradschools.com
www.aacn.nche.edu (American Association of Colleges of Nursing)

For general career change information:

www.jobhuntersbible.com

For information on specific job openings, posting your resume, and other activities for the general public:

www.careerbuilder.com
www.monster.com
www.headhunter.net
www.cruelworld.com

For special areas:

www.military.com/careers
www.idealist.org (nonprofit organizations)
www.miracleworkers.com (human service jobs)
www.voa.org (Volunteers of America)
www.disasterrelief.org
http://imc-la.org (International Medical Corps)

Some useful directories:

www.yellowonline (United States yellow pages)
www.ahd.com (American hospital directory)
www.weddles.com/associations (directory of trade associations)

If you find that the website has changed for any of the organizations mentioned, enter the name in one of these search engines:

www.metacrawler.com
www.yahoo.com
www.excite.com
www.altavista.com
www.dogpile.com

appendix C

State Boards of Nursing

For a link to State Boards of Nursing and on-line information:
www.ncsbn.org/files/boards/boardscontact.asp

To contact your State Board of Nursing otherwise:

Alabama Board of Nursing
RSA Plaza, Suite 250
770 Washington Avenue
Montgomery, AL 36130
(334) 242-4060

Alaska Board of Nursing
Division of Occupational Licensing
3601 C Street, Suite 722
Anchorage, AK 99503
(907) 269-8161

American Samoa Health Services
Regulatory Board
LBJ Tropical Medical Center
Pago Pago, AS 96799
(684) 633-1222

Arizona Board of Nursing
1651 East Morten Avenue, Suite 210
Phoenix, AZ 85020
(602) 331-8111

Arkansas State Board of Nursing
University Tower Building
1123 South University Avenue, Suite 800
Little Rock, AR 72204
(501) 686-2700

California Board of Registered Nursing
400 R Street, Suite 4030
Sacramento, CA 95814
(916) 322-3350

Colorado Board of Nursing
1560 Broadway, Suite 800
Denver, CO 80202
(303) 894-2430

Commonwealth Board of Nurse Examiners
Public Health Center
PO Box 1458
Saipan, MP 96950
(670) 234-8950

Connecticut Board of Examiners for Nursing
410 Capital Avenue, MS 13ADJ
PO Box 430308
Hartford, CT 06134
(860) 509-7624

Delaware Board of Nursing
861 Silver Lake Boulevard
Cannon Building, Suite 203
Dover, DE 19904
(302) 739-4522

District of Columbia Board of Nursing
Department of Health
825 North Capitol Street, NE, 2nd floor
Washington, DC 20002
(202) 442-4778

Florida State Board of Nursing
4080 Woodcock Drive, Suite 202
Jacksonville, FL 32207
(904) 858-6940

Georgia Board of Nursing
237 Coliseum Drive
Macon, GA 31217
(912) 207-1640

Guam Board of Nurse Examiners
PO Box 2816
1304 East Sunset Boulevard
Barrgada, GU 96913
011-671-475-0251

Hawaii Board of Nursing
Professional and Vocational Licensing Division
PO Box 3469
Honolulu, HI 96801
(808) 586-3000

Idaho Board of Nursing
280 North 8th Street, Suite 210
Boise, ID 83720
(208) 334-3110

Illinois Department of Professional Regulation
James R. Thompson Center
100 West Randolph, Suite 9-300
Chicago, IL 60601
(312) 814-2715

Indiana State Board of Nursing
402 West Washington Street, Room W041
Indianapolis, IN 46204
(317) 232-2960

Iowa Board of Nursing
400 SW 8th Street, Suite B
Des Moines, IA 50309
(515) 281-3255

Kansas Board of Nursing
900 SW Jackson, Suite 551-S
Topeka, KS 66612
(785) 296-4929

Kentucky State Board of Nursing
312 Whittington Parkway, Suite 300
Louisville, KY 40222
(502) 329-7000

Louisiana State Board of Nursing
3510 North Causeway Boulevard, Suite 501
Metairie, LA 70003
(504) 838-5332

Maine State Board of Nursing
158 State House Station
Augusta, ME 04433
(207) 287-1133

Maryland Board of Nursing
4140 Patterson Avenue
Baltimore, MD 21215
(410) 585-1900

Massachusetts Board of Registration in Nursing
239 Causeway Street
Boston, MA 02114
(617) 727-9961

Michigan CIS/Office of Health Services
Ottawa Towers North
611 West Ottawa, 4th Floor
Lansing, MI 48933
(517) 373-9102

Minnesota Board of Nursing
2829 University Avenue SE
Minneapolis, MN 55414
(612) 617-2270

Mississippi Board of Nursing
1935 Lakeland Drive, Suite B
Jackson, MS 39216
(601) 987-4188

Missouri State Board of Nursing
PO Box 656
3605 Missouri Boulevard
Jefferson City, MO 65102
(314) 751-0681

Montana State Board of Nursing
301 South Park
Helena, MT 59620
(406) 444-2071

Nebraska Health and Human Services System
Department of Regulation and Licensure, Nursing Section
301 Centennial Mall South
PO Box 94986
Lincoln, NE 68509
(402) 471-4376

Nevada State Board of Nursing
1755 East Plumb Lane, Suite 260
Reno, NV 89502
(775) 688-2620

New Hampshire Board of Nursing
78 Regional Drive, Building B
Concord, NH 03302
(603) 271-2323

New Jersey Board of Nursing
124 Halsey Street, 6th Floor
PO Box 45010
Newark, NJ 07101
(973) 504-6586

New Mexico Board of Nursing
4206 Louisiana Boulevard, NE, Suite A
Albuquerque, NM 87109
(505) 841-8340

New York State Board of Nursing
89 Washington Avenue
Education Building, 2nd Floor West Wing
Albany, NY 12234
(518) 473-6999

North Carolina Board of Nursing
3724 National Drive, Suite 201
Raleigh, NC 27612
(919) 782-3211

North Dakota Board of Nursing
919 South 7th Street, Suite 504
Bismarck, ND 58504
(701) 328-9777

Ohio Board of Nursing
17 South High Street, Suite 400
Columbus, OH 43215
(614) 466-3947

Oklahoma Board of Nursing, Registration and Education
2915 North Classen Boulevard, Suite 524
Oklahoma City, OK 73106
(405) 962-1800

Oregon State Board of Nursing
800 NE Oregon Street, Suite 465
Portland, OR 97232
(503) 731-4745

Pennsylvania State Board of Nursing
124 Pine Street
PO Box 2649
Harrisburg, PA 17101
(717) 783-7142

Commonwealth of Puerto Rico
Board of Nurse Examiners
800 Roberto H. Todd Avenue, Room 202
Santurce, PR 00908
(787) 725-8161

Rhode Island Board of Nursing
105 Cannon Building, Room
Three Capitol Hill
Providence, RI 02908
(401) 222-5700

South Carolina State Board of Nursing
110 Centerview Drive, Suite 202
Columbia, SC 29210
(803) 896-4550

South Dakota Board of Nursing
4300 South Louise Avenue, Suite C-1
Sioux Falls, SD 57106
(605) 362-2760

Tennessee State Board of Nursing
426 Fifth Avenue North
1st Floor, Cordell Hull Building
Nashville, TN 37247
(615) 532-5166

Texas Board of Nurse Examiners
333 Guadalupe, Suite 3-460
Austin, TX 78701
(512) 305-7400

Utah State Board of Nursing
Heber M. Wells Building, 4th Floor
160 East 300 South
Salt Lake City, UT 84111
(801) 530-6628

Vermont State Board of Nursing
109 State Street
Montpelier, VT 05609
(802) 828-2396

Virgin Islands Board of Nurse Licensure
Veterans Drive Station
St. Thomas, VI 00803
(340) 776-7397

Virginia State Board of Nursing
6606 West Broad Street, 4th Floor
Richmond, VA 23230
(804) 662-9909

Washington State Nursing Care
Quality Assurance Commission
Department of Health
1300 Quince Street SE
Olympia, WA 98504
(360) 236-4740

West Virginia Board of Examiners for Registered Professional Nurses
101 Dee Drive
Charleston, WV 25311
(304) 558-3596

Wisconsin Department of Regulation and Licensing
1400 East Washington Avenue
PO Box 8935
Madison, WI 53708
(608) 266-0145

Wyoming State Board of Nursing
2020 Carey Avenue, Suite 110
Cheyenne, WY 82002
(307) 777-7601

appendix D

Specialty Certification Boards

For a link to the Web sites of many specialty certification boards go to: www.nursingcenter.com/career/certification.cfm

The American Nurses Credentialing Center should be contacted for information about the certifications that follow. You can reach them by phone or fax at: American Nurses Credentialing Center 1-800-284-2378; fax: (202) 554-2262. For the Credentialing Center of the American Nurses Association on-line: www.nursingworld.org.

Acute Care Nurse Practitioner (CS)
Adult Nurse Practitioner (CS)
Cardiac Rehabilitation Nurse (C)
Case Management (CM)
Clinical Specialist in Adult Psychiatric Mental Health Nursing (CS)
Clinical Specialist in Child and Adolescent Psychiatric and Mental Health Nursing (CS)
Clinical Specialist in Community Health Nursing (CS)
Clinical Specialist in Gerontological Nursing (CS)
Clinical Specialist in Home Health Nursing (CS)
Clinical Specialist in Medical-Surgical Nursing (CS)
College Health Nurse (C)
Community Health Nurse (C)
Family Nurse Practitioner (CS)
General Nursing Practice (C)

Gerontological Nurse Practitioner (CS)
Gerontological Nurse (C)
Home Health Nurse (C)
Informatics Nurse (C)
Medical-Surgical Nurse (C)
Nursing Administration (CNA), (CNAA)
Nursing Continuing Education/Staff Development (C)
Pediatric Nurse Practitioner (CS)
Pediatric Nurse (C)
Perinatal Nurse (C)
Psychiatric and Mental Health Nurse (C)
School Nurse (C)
School Nurse Practitioner (C)

The following certifications are obtained through National Certification Corporation for the Obstetric, Gynecologic and Neonatal, Nursing Specialties, PO Box 11082, Chicago, IL 60611:

Inpatient Obstetric Nurse (RNC)
Low Risk Neonatal Nurse (RNC)
Maternal Newborn Nurse (RNC)
Neonatal Intensive Care Nurse (RNC)
Neonatal Nurse Practitioner (RNC)
Women's Health Nursing (RNC)

Other certification areas are listed, along with the appropriate contact information.

Addictions Nursing (CARN)
Center for Nursing Education and Testing
601 Pavonia Avenue, Suite 204
Jersey City, NJ 07306
(201) 217-9083

Case Manager (CCM)
Commission for Case Manager Certification
1835 Rohlwing Road, #E
Rolling Meadows, IL 60008
(847) 818-0292

Childbirth Educators (ACCE)
Lamaze International
1200 19th Street NW, Suite 300
Washington, DC 20036

Critical Care Nursing (CCRN)
Critical Care Nurse Specialist/AACN Certification Corporation
101 Columbia
Aliso Viejo, CA 92656-1491

Diabetes Educators (DE)
National Certification Board for Diabetes Educators
435 North Michigan Avenue, Suite 1717
Chicago, IL 60611

Emergency Nursing (CEN)
Board for Certification for Emergency Nursing
216 Higgins Road
Park Ridge, IL 60068-5736

Gastroenterology (CGN), (CGRN)
Certifying Board of Gastroenterology Nurses and Associates, Inc.
3525 North Ellicott Mills Drive, Suite N
Ellicott City, MD 21043

Healthcare Quality (CPHQ)
Healthcare Quality Certification Board
Box 1880
San Gabriel, CA 91778
(847) 375-4700

HIV/AIDS Nursing (ACRN)
HIV/AIDS Nursing Certification Board
c/o Professional Testing Corporation
1211 Avenue of Americas, 15th Floor
New York, NY 10036

Holistic Nursing (HNC)
American Holistic Nurses' Certification Corporation
Box 2130
Flagstaff, AZ 86003

Hospice and Palliative Nurse (CRNH)
National Board for Certification of Hospice Nurses
211 North Whitfield Street, Suite 375
Pittsburgh, PA 15206
(412) 361-2470

Infection Control (CIC)
Certification Board of Infection Control and Epidemiology, Inc.
4700 West Lake Avenue
Glenview, IL 60025
(847) 375-4830

Intravenous Nursing (CRNI)
Intravenous Nurses Certification Corporation
Fresh Pond Square
10 Fawcett Street
Cambridge, MA 02138

Lactation Consultant (IBCLC)
International Board of Lactation Consultant Examiners
Box 2348
Falls Church, VA 22042

Legal Nurse Consulting (LNCC)
American LNC Board
4700 West Lake Avenue
Glenview, IL 60025
(847) 375-4700

Nephrology Nursing (CPDN)
Peritoneal Dialysis Nursing
Board of Nephrology Examiners, Nursing and Technology (BONENT)
PO Box 15945-282
Lenexa, KS 66285

Neuroscience Nursing (CNRN)
American Board of Neuroscience Nursing Professional Examination Service
224 North Des Plaines, Suite 601
Chicago, IL 60661

Nurse Administration Long-Term Care (CDONA/LTC)
CDONA/LTC Certification Registration
10999 Reed Hartman Highway, Suite 233
Cincinnati, OH 45242

Nurse Anesthetist (CRNA)
Council on Certification of Nurse Anesthetists
222 South Prospect Avenue
Park Ridge, IL 60068

Nurse Midwifery and Midwifery (CNM), (CM)
ACNM Certification Council, Inc.
8401 Corporate Drive, Suite 630
Landover, MD 20785
(301) 459-1321

Occupational Health Nursing (COHN/CM), (COHN-S/CM)
American Board for Occupational Health Nurses, Inc.
201 East Ogden, Suite 114
Hinsdale, IL 60521

Oncology Nursing (OCN/AOCN)
Oncology Nursing Certification Corporation
501 Holiday Drive
Pittsburgh, PA 15220

Ophthalmic Nursing (CRNO)
National Certifying Board for Ophthalmic Registered Nurses
655 Beach Street
Box 19303
San Francisco, CA 94119

Orthopaedic Nursing (ONC)
Orthopaedic Nurses Certification Board
East Holly Avenue Box 56
Pitman, NJ 08071

Pain Management (FAAPM)
American Academy of Pain Management
13947 Mono Way #A
Sonora, CA 95370

Pediatric Nursing (CPN) (General Pediatric Nursing)
National Certification Board of Pediatric Nurse Practitioners and Nurses
800 South Frederick Avenue, Suite 104
Gaithersburg, MD 20877

Pediatric Oncology (CPON)
Certification Corporation of Pediatric Oncology Nurses
7700 West Lake Avenue
Glenview, IL 60025
(847) 375-4700

Perianesthesia Nursing (CPAN), (CAPA) (Certified Post Anesthesia Nurse)
American Board of Perianesthesia Nursing Certification, Inc.
475 Riverside Drive, 7th Floor
New York, NY 10115
(800) 6AB-PANC

Perioperative Nursing (CNOR)
National Certification Board of Perioperative Nursing
2170 South Parker Road, Suite 295
Denver, CO 80231

Plastic and Reconstructive Surgical Nursing (CPSN)
Plastic Surgical Nursing Certification Board
East Holly Avenue Box 56
Pitman, NJ 08071

Rehabilitation Nursing (CRRN), (CRRN-A)
Rehabilitation Nursing Certification Board
4700 West Lake Avenue
Glenview, IL 60025
(800) 229-7530

School Nursing (CSN)
National Board for Certification of School Nurses, Inc.
Box 1300
Scarborough, ME 04070

Urology Nursing (CURN, CUA, CUNP, CUCNS, CUPA)
Certification Board for Urologic Nurses and Associates
East Holly Avenue, Box 56
Pitman, NJ 08071

appendix E

Small Business Administration Regional Offices

For on-line information about the Small Business Administration assistance in your area: www.SBA.gov

To contact the regional office for your state

Region 1. Massachusetts, Vermont, Connecticut, Rhode Island, Maine, New Hampshire

Small Business Administration
Boston Regional Office
10 Causeway Street, Suite 812
Boston, MA 02222
(617) 565-8415

Region 2. New Jersey, New York, Puerto Rico

Small Business Administration
New York Regional Office
26 Federal Plaza, Suite 3108
New York, NY 10278
(212) 264-1450

Region 3. Pennsylvania, Virginia, Delaware, District of Columbia, Maryland, West Virginia

Small Business Administration
Philadelphia Regional Office
900 Market Street, 5th Floor
Philadelphia, PA 19107
(215) 580-2722

Region 4. Georgia, Mississippi, Florida, Kentucky, Alabama, North Carolina

South Carolina, Tennessee

Small Business Administration
Atlanta Regional Office
1720 Peachtree Road, NW, Suite 496
Atlanta, GA 30309
(404) 347-4999

Region 5. Illinois, Minnesota, Michigan, Ohio, Wisconsin, Indiana

Small Business Administration
Chicago Regional Office
500 West Madison Street, Suite 1240
Chicago, IL 60661
(312) 353-0357

Region 6. Texas, Arkansas, Louisiana, Oklahoma, New Mexico

Small Business Administration
Dallas Regional Office
4300 Amon Carter Boulevard, Suite 108
Fort Worth, TX 76155
(817) 885-6581

Region 7. Missouri, Iowa, Nebraska, Kansas

Small Business Administration
Kansas City Regional Office
323 West Eighth Street, Suite 307
Kansas City, MO 64105
(816) 374-6380

Region 8. Colorado, North Dakota, South Dakota, Utah, Montana, Wyoming

Small Business Administration
Denver Regional Office
721 19th Street, Suite 400
Denver, CO 80202
(303) 844-0500

Region 9. California, Nevada, Hawaii, Arizona, Guam

Small Business Administration
San Francisco Regional Office
455 Market Street, Suite 2200
San Francisco, CA 94105
(415) 744-2118

Region 10. Washington, Alaska, Oregon, Idaho

Small Business Administration
Seattle Regional Office
1200 Sixth Avenue, Suite 1805
Seattle, WA 98101
(206) 553-5676

Index